Direct Your

Mind

How to Steer Your Mind to Work For You Rather Than Against You

Adam Khan

Published by: YouMe Works
Printed in the United States

ISBN-13: 978-1623810078
ISBN-10: 1623810078

Table of Contents

Introduction

Charlie has a problem. He has been trying to get his carpet-cleaning business off the ground, but it has been taking longer than he expected. He has a lot of debt on his credit cards, just stringing himself along until his business starts making enough money.

The economy entered a recession and some people are putting off getting their carpets cleaned. And then yesterday, one of his credit card companies dropped a bomb on him: They are raising the minimum monthly payment. He will suddenly owe more per month on his credit cards than he is able to pay.

He has some decisions to make, but first he needs to get his mind to calm down so he can think. His first instinct is to panic. This is a disaster. This is a catastrophe!

Charlie is going to have to do something. But the most important element in his response to his problem is how he thinks about it. The way he thinks about it will determine what he does and how well he does it. The way he thinks about it will determine whether he takes his time and thinks it through or panics and does something stupid. The way he thinks about it makes all the difference.

And when I say "think" I mean "talking to himself." I know visualizing things is also called *thinking*, but that's a kind of thinking for another book. This book is about how we *talk* to ourselves, because the clearest, easiest and most definite way to direct your mind is by talking to yourself.

So what is the best way to talk to yourself? What's the best way to direct your mind so it works for you rather than against you? What kind of thinking is going to help Charlie deal with his problem?

There are a number of different ways to talk to yourself, and some are better than others. For example, Charlie could reassure himself. He could tell himself, "It's going to be fine. It'll turn out okay."

Another way he could talk to himself is to give himself advice or instructions. He could tell himself, "Okay, just stay calm and don't do anything rash. Let's just think about this."

Another possible way to talk to himself would be to put himself down. "I'm such a loser. I can't believe I was stupid enough to get into this mess."

Or he could ask himself a question. "How do I want this all to turn out?"

Of all the possible ways to talk to yourself, asking yourself a question is the most powerful. Questions direct your mind and set trains of thought into motion. Questions are generative. They *generate* thought. And because they are so powerful it really makes a difference to pay attention to the questions you ask yourself and make sure they are good questions.

Charlie could ask himself a bad question, such as, "Why is this happening to me?" Or, "How could I have been so stupid?" Or, "What if I have to declare bankruptcy? What if I can't start another business because I have no credit?"

Those are unproductive questions. What-if questions and "why" questions put the mind in a spin and don't help. "Why am I such a loser?" "Why does stuff like this always happen to me?" "Why can't I ever get anything right?" These questions are poor quality.

What makes a high-quality question? What makes a question a *good* question? The answer is simple. A good question leads to a good *result*. It focuses your attention on something that makes you *effective*. It directs your mind to something that helps you successfully handle the situation. A question is *good* if it leads to a good outcome.

Bad question: What if they don't like me?

Better question: What is something I could do right now that would make me more likable?

Bad question: What if I fail to accomplish my goal?

Better question: What's the most important thing I could do to accomplish my goal?

Bad question: What if I go bankrupt?

Better question: What do I need to know before I make a decision?

A high-quality question is one that produces an end-result you desire. To come up with a good question, ask yourself, "What result do I want?" That's the root question, and should always be the first question you ask in any situation. What do you want?

And when you decide on a result you want, ask yourself, "What question can I ponder that would help me achieve that result?"

Don't settle for the first thing that pops into your head! *Think* about it. Make a list on paper. Force yourself to come up with ten or more possible questions. Then choose what you think is the *best* question — the one you think will produce the best result — and practice asking yourself that question. Literally *practice*. Ask the question many times. Get used to asking it. Make it familiar and comfortable and automatic.

I've experimented a lot with questions. In the chapters that follow, I will share with you some of the best questions to use. You can and should, of course, come up with your own questions. But when you don't know what question to use, try one of mine. They have already proven themselves. But before I share those questions, I want you to be sure you know what to do with them, or with any questions you use.

First decide what *result* you want. Then ask, "What question can I ponder that might help me achieve that result?"

There are certain times, certain situations, when it would help to ask yourself a particular question. So practice asking your question at those times.

For example, when Katie is preparing for an interview, she doesn't want her mind to be occupied by the questions that naturally come to her: "What if they don't want me?" and "What if I make a fool of myself in the interview?" She is fully aware that those questions don't put her in the best frame of mind to have a successful interview.

She decides a good question to have in mind is, "How can I help these people?" That'll put her in just the right attitude for an interview. That's a question that might produce a good result.

So after she makes an appointment for the interview, she ponders the question. And on the day of the interview, while she's getting dressed for it, she asks herself that question. She ponders it. When her mind wanders, she comes back to her chosen question. And in the car, on the way to the interview, she thinks about it some more, trying to think of ways she can help her future employers if they hire her.

Whenever her mind drifts to her worries, she asks herself, "But how can I *help* these people?" And even walking into the interview, she is wondering how she can help them.

What do you think would be the difference between Katie sitting down for an interview wondering, "What if they don't want me?" versus sitting down wondering, "How can I help these people?" What kind of difference would she have in her *attitude?* In her demeanor? In her level of stress hormones? In her *focus* — outward versus inward?

I think you can see it would be a large and visibly obvious difference. The second question would make her more effective in the interview. The second question is more likely to lead to a good result.

You can also practice questions for certain situations in your imagination. If Charlie is having a difficulty with Jed, his 16 year-old son, for example, and he keeps losing his temper, he can decide he wants to stay calm and reasonable. Then the question is, what question can he ponder that would help him stay calm and reasonable?

How about this one: "What does Jed really want?" Charlie wants that question to be going through his mind next time he's in an argument with Jed. So he practices his question. He imagines talking to Jed, and then asks that question to himself while he pictures the scene. This associates the question with that circumstance.

Charlie can also remember previous arguments, and while he is remembering, he can ask his question, "What does Jed really want?"

With a little practice, the next time Charlie is talking to Jed, the question will automatically come to Charlie's mind, and will help lead to a good result — hopefully, it will lead to Charlie staying calm and reasonable in the conversation.

If the question does not lead to the result you want, what should you do? Come up with a better question, of course.

The reason questions are so useful is that they *drive* your mind to produce answers, and often that drive, that power, can be used to do a tremendous amount of good.

It is especially useful to replace *bad* questions you are already asking with *good* questions. For example, a typical question people ask when bad stuff happens is, "Why me? What did I do to deserve this?" It is a question that doesn't lead to a good result, yet there are plenty of questions you could ask in those circumstances that would benefit you.

The quality of the questions you ask makes a tremendous difference. Ask yourself over and over, "What is wrong with me?" and your mind will search for answers, finding one after another. Because our brains are driven to answer questions, if you ask this question, you *will* come up with answers. Do the answers help you?

Compare that question with this one: "How can I prevent this from ever happening again?" Someone who ponders *this* question will get much more productive answers and won't create anywhere close to the same amount of negative emotion.

The principle is simple: Ask yourself a good question. That's how to direct your mind so it works for you rather than against you.

Think about the questions you ask, and come up with good ones. And when you ask a good question, *keep asking it*. Any answer you get is only one possible answer. Keep *asking* and you'll keep getting new answers. The more answers you have to a good question, the better.

If it's a good question, it's a good thought to practice. Make that good question familiar and comfortable so it comes to mind easily and often.

One of the advantages of asking questions is the lack of force in it. You are not *trying*. You're not *making yourself* "be positive." You are simply pondering a question honestly. And it has a real impact.

Asking yourself a question is the best way to direct your mind. Of the many ways to talk to yourself, asking a question is the most powerful. Now we're going to investigate some good questions.

You will probably create your own questions tailored to your specific circumstances and your personality. But when you want a good question you can start using without having to think up one, use one of the following twenty-five questions to ask yourself. Let's start with one of the best: What are you grateful for?

What Am I Grateful For?

You can come up with different answers to this question every day, and if you did, you'd be happier, according to the research. One study on gratefulness asked the participants to merely write for five minutes a day in a diary — to write about what they were grateful for. It made them measurably happier, and their improved moods lasted for a considerable time afterward.

Five minutes a day? Why would such a small thing have such a strong impact?

When you ask what you're grateful for, you're using the power of comparison. To feel grateful for your good health you would have to compare your health to a worse state of health.

Also, your brain has a negative bias. It tends to focus on what's wrong. The question, "What am I grateful for?" bypasses the negative bias, or uses it to your advantage rather than using it against you.

Ask the question, find an answer, and ask it again. What *else* are you grateful for? I sometimes do it using a timer. I set the timer for five minutes and write a list of things I am grateful for, and I always feel significantly better afterward. At first I was surprised how easy it was to fill a page with things I'm grateful for. I hardly have to try. I write nonstop, and have a pretty big list at the end of five minutes. This is so simple and so powerful I really urge you to try this one. It's not work. It's not a chore. It feels good.

Another variation that works pretty well is: What could I feel great about if I wanted to?

Another variation: What do I appreciate about (a particular person)? This is a good one to write down. When you're done, give it to the person, or even go so far as to read it to them.

When you would like to direct your mind to something positive, when you'd like to feel better, when you would like to be aware of what is great about your life, ask yourself, "What am I grateful for?" It works every time.

If I Was Happy About This, What Would I Be Thinking About It?

Sometimes it's easier to ask this version: "If someone else, more capable and wiser than me was happy about this, what would *that* person be thinking about it?"

Your car breaks down, it's pouring rain, and you're late for an important interview. Of course this is miserable. One possible and perfectly understandable reaction you could have is to throw a fit of rage. To freak out. To cry, scream, curse the gods.

But when you're all done and you've made your phone calls and you're waiting for the tow truck to arrive, you can explore your mind by imagining this same set of circumstances, but imagine that somehow you are happy about it. What would you have to be thinking to be happy about it?

Have I gone overboard here? Is this pie-in-the-sky positive thinking on steroids? How can *anybody* be happy in those circumstances? Why would anyone even *want* to be happy in those circumstances?

The why is easy: You'll feel better and get more done. It will do you no good at all to feel miserable. What's done is done. You are in those circumstances, no matter how you feel about them. And negative emotions are generally hard on you. Anytime you can remove unnecessary negative emotions from your life, you've benefited your health.

And you will respond to things better, you'll be more creative at solving problems, and you will treat people you love with more care and respect if you feel better. The way you feel has real consequences.

So that takes care of the *why*. Let's look at the *how*. How could a person feel happy under those circumstances? Broken-down car, rain, late for meeting. You *can't* do it by forcing yourself, I can tell you that. You cannot *force* yourself to feel good. Why? Because forcing yourself doesn't feel good.

But you could have a different perspective on your situation. You could look at it differently, and thereby feel differently. You could be only mildly upset about it, you could be not bothered at all about it, or you could actually feel happy — you could feel *good* about your circumstances. All it takes is a little creativity on your part.

12

Your answers to the question depend on you and your circumstances. If I was in that circumstance, for example (with the rain and late for an appointment, etc.), these are some of the things I would have to be thinking if I was happy about it: "I'm glad this happened to me and not my wife. I'm glad this happened when I was in the slow lane and could get off the road without causing an accident. It will be interesting to find out how the interviewer responds to my missing the meeting (sort of like a test of character), and it might make a good real-life illustration to use on the rescheduled interview. I'm glad this happened because since I've been sitting here waiting for the tow truck I've had time to reflect on the fact that I was running late already, and perhaps my own greed needs to be curbed — I'm trying to stuff too much into my days and I'm past the point where it is fun. I need to slow the pace and make it more fun. I'm glad this event has given me time to reflect and readjust my priorities."

And so on. You get the idea. The more you think about it, the more there is to be happy about. It's also true that the more you think about it, the more things you could think of to be *miserable* about, but the question is: Which do you choose? Because it really is *your* choice, and your choice will have consequences one way or the other.

Another alternative way to ask this question is: "What would I like to feel about this?" And then after you get the answer to that one, ask: "What would I have to think about it in order to feel that way?"

I once had an appointment with the dentist for the following day, and I wasn't looking forward to it. So I asked, "What do I want to feel?" Of course, my answer was, I wanted to be glad I was going to the dentist, or at least no longer feel dread.

My next question was, *"What would I have to think* that would make me feel good in these circumstances?"

One of my answers was, "I would have to think I was grateful that I live in a time and place that has dentists to take care of my teeth." I thought about other places and times (all of human history except the very recent) when people got painful cavities, lost their teeth, and suffered tremendous agony because they did not have dentists, because dentistry hadn't even been invented, or it was only for the rich or whatever, and here I was ungratefully wishing I didn't have to go.

And the truth is, I *didn't* have to go. It was my privilege to be able to go. I felt glad about going, and no longer dreaded it.

And I changed my attitude by beginning with the simple question, "What would I *like* to feel?"

Okay, you have a bad feeling, but what would you *like* to feel? And then go on from there and ponder the question, "What could I think about the situation that would result in that feeling?"

Also note that I changed the way I looked at it and felt better *without fooling myself* or trying to believe something I didn't really believe, or trying to *force* myself to feel any particular way. I felt better honestly and genuinely by looking at the real situation with a broader perspective than I had been using.

It's important not to do this questioning with a forcing attitude, or in a hurry. Just ponder it like you're daydreaming. Just wonder about it. Imagine you're in a hammock drinking a lemonade. Imagine it's a lazy summer afternoon and you have absolutely nothing to do but enjoy the cool breeze. Imagine you've got all day to lie around and daydream. Then ask the question in a relaxed, curious way. Imagine you're pondering the question for your own amusement and nothing more.

Questions direct your mind. And *this* question is a great way to generate whole new trains of thought that will lead you to better feelings (and better health): If I was happy about this, what would I be thinking about it?

What Did I Do Right Today?

One night I was getting ready for bed and I felt disappointed in myself. It had been a busy day but I didn't feel like I'd done much to advance my goals, and I did a couple of things poorly. I didn't want to end the day feeling down. Days like that I feel like I'm spinning my wheels and going nowhere. I feel frustrated and don't look forward to tomorrow. Have you ever felt that way? Have you ever wished you had a way to bring yourself out of it?

Well, from now on, you'll have something you can use. I invented a technique that night and I've used it many times since, and it works every time to raise my spirits and make me feel strong again, looking forward to another day.

I asked myself, "What did I do today that was right?" As soon as I asked it, I thought of something.

Earlier that day I was going to say something in anger, and I held my tongue. "That was a good thing to do," I thought to myself. And I already felt better. I had done at least one thing right.

But I didn't stop there. I asked it again. What else did I do right today? After only a minute's thought or less, I thought of another one. There were three small items on my desk I'd been meaning to do but not getting around to, and I got them done that day.

I felt better still. The day wasn't a total loss. Not at all. And even though I did a couple things poorly, I had also done a couple things right, and this made me feel better.

I asked the question again a few more times and went to sleep feeling relaxed and satisfied, looking forward to a new day.

If this technique did nothing more than make me feel better, it would have been worthwhile. An improved mood is a definite asset. But the question does something else that may be even more valuable: It made me look into my day to see which actions I took were the most valuable.

Each right thing you do is something you do voluntarily — you have a choice in whether to do it or not.

By paying special attention to which ones are the truly good choices, you clarify your goals and moral principles. You clarify what you think is good. You clarify what you want more of. This clarity has practical, long-term benefits.

Ask yourself the question tonight. What did you do today that helped you achieve your most important goals? What did you do right today? What did you do that you can feel good about? Think of something, even a small thing. Enjoy it for a moment, and then ask the question again. What else? And what else? It's an excellent exercise to help you feel good more often and increase your ability to accomplish your goals.

Give yourself credit for what you do right or well. A variation on this question is, "What would I do differently if I could do the day over?" And then "What am I really glad I did today?" Very helpful. Very productive.

Another version is: "What did I do today that was productive and what was a waste of my time?"

Another version is: What did I do that makes me feel proud of myself?

These are all questions to help solve a common problem: Neglecting to take credit for what you do *right* and focusing your attention on what you do *wrong*. The human brain's naturally negative bias gives this tendency to nearly everyone.

The simple solution is to start taking credit for the things you do right. Ask yourself what you're doing right, and keep asking, getting more and more answers. It is amazingly relaxing. It is a relief to know you've done *some* things right, and it makes you more aware of what you consider to be "right."

The question is a great one to ask at the end of the day, but you can ask it any time. In the car on the way home from work, for example, ask yourself, "What did I do right today?"

What can you take credit for? Go ahead and feel good.

Bragging may be a social blunder, but giving yourself legitimate credit in the privacy of your own mind, for the good things you do, is healthy, it feels good, and it boosts and helps maintain feelings of motivation (so it will help you accomplish your goals in the long run).

What CAN I Change?

One of the many interesting findings in the research on depression is that the most depressing assumption you can make is: *This is permanent.* If you think something bad is permanent and cannot be changed, it is one of the most — if not the most — demoralizing thought you can have.

If you are mistaken about the permanence, it is of enormous benefit to recognize your mistake. The moment of recognition can restore your morale immediately.

But sometimes you will realize that you were *not* mistaken. You assumed something was permanent and you were right. Then what?

Then the question is, "What *can* I change?"

To answer that question, however, you must first know the answer to a pre-question: *What do I want?*

So for example, you're trying to sell pet rocks, and you're not selling very many, so you argue with your negative thoughts on paper and one of your negative thoughts is: *The fad is over.* That is a permanent explanation of your setback. And let's say you realize you are correct about this, and you realize no matter what you do, you may never be able to revive the fad. You feel demoralized by this realization. Now what?

The question is first, *What do you want?* Let's say you want to have a successful business selling something.

Then the second question is: *What can I change?* Of course, you can change what you sell. If you want to be successful at selling something, it doesn't have to be pet rocks. You could change *what* you sell, the *way* you sell it, change the way the rocks look, etc. What *can* you change?

When you find yourself fixated by the negative bias — when all you can see is what you *can't* change — pull this question out of your pocket and ask it and keep asking it and don't let it go until you've found some good answers.

Does This Help My Goal?

In the movie, *Terminator 2: Judgment Day*, John (the kid) finds out the bad Terminator is probably going to kill his mom. John wants to find her and warn her. The good Terminator says, "Negative. It is not a mission priority."

The kid starts yelling. The good terminator (Arnold) says, "This does not help our mission."

Throughout the movie, Arnold plays a machine that has only one goal and never lets go of it, never gets distracted from it, never comes up with a new goal, and never gets discouraged by setbacks. During the whole movie, he evaluates every possible action with only one criteria: Does it help his goal or doesn't it? If it doesn't, he has no time for it. He doesn't waste any time fuming about someone else's behavior. He doesn't waste any time thinking about what he "should have" done. He just stays on his purpose.

Of course, the Terminator is a machine. But imagine how much you could accomplish with that kind of clear focus. This question, asked all the time, every day, would help you do that (without becoming a cold machine yourself, because you have several goals, including maintaining good relationships and being happy).

One of the values of "motivational material" like success books and seminars is that they get you thinking about your goals. The simple focus on your goal is motivating.

That means if this question was on your mind a lot, you'd feel motivated more often.

In a course my wife, Klassy Evans, used to teach, she demonstrated the motivational power of keeping your eye on the goal with a little help from the audience. She asked for two volunteers to come up to the front of the room and let her make them feel bad. Let's go into the courseroom now and listen to Klassy do the demonstration. The following was transcribed from one of the courses:

"I need two people. The only requirement is that you are wearing comfortable shoes. You? Good. Thank you. Come on up. And you? Excellent. Now [speaking to the two volunteers] I'd like you to look at the audience and find someone who would be a good match for you in a tug of war — and who is also wearing comfortable shoes.

"Okay [to the audience] these two people [referring to the first two volunteers] are going to represent you in your life. You're going to see what your life looks like. You two volunteers stand here and here and face that wall across the room [the wall to the right of the stage from the audiences' perspective; the volunteers are to the left of center-stage].

"That wall will represent a goal of yours," says Klassy. "You're going to try to reach it while the person behind you tries to stop you. They are the barriers to your goal.

"Not just yet, but in a little while I'm going to ask you two barriers to come up behind them and put your arms around their waist, and be a drag on them while they try to reach their goal.

[She turns to the audience]: "We all have things that hold us back. If we didn't, we'd just go get what we wanted. So if you don't have what you want, it's because something is acting as a barrier to hold you back.

[Speaking to the two people (the barriers) that the first two volunteers have chosen]: "You two barriers, we're going to do the demonstration twice and I want you to stay consistent. Hold them back equally the first and second time because I want the difference to be a result in *them*, not because of something you are doing differently, okay? [They nod].

[Speaking to the goal-seekers — the first two volunteers]: "With your permission, I'm now going to bring you down. Then when I say, 'Go for what you want,' I want you to start moving toward your goal, represented by this wall [the wall to the right of center stage].

"But first, I'd like you to think of some bad news you've heard lately...[Klassy gives them time to think of some. When it looks like they've both found something, she continues]:

"Think of a mistake you've made...

"Now think of something good in your life...

"and realize it's not going to last...

"Think of something bad in your life...

"and realize it's probably permanent...

"and you're going to have to deal with it for the rest of your life...

"Think about a weakness you have, a fault you have, something that holds you back...

"Think of something that stands in your way and prevents you from getting what you want...

"and realize it is more than you can handle...

"Add up all the barriers you can think of that stand in your way...

"and all your personal weaknesses...

"and come to grips with the fact that your goal is completely hopeless...

"You'll save yourself a lot of heartache if you just give up now...

"Now I'd like the barriers to come up behind you and put their arms around your waist and interlace their fingers. And I'd like you to look down at their hands and keep looking at their hands, feeling the strength in their arms. Keep your attention on the barriers, and think about all the things that the arms represent: the barriers, your weaknesses, the hopelessness of the task. In your thoughts, I want you to hear what you tell yourself about all your failures and shortcomings and everything that's wrong with you. When you feel down, what do you say to yourself about yourself?

"Remember vividly all the times you have failed..."

"Keep looking down at the hands and be aware of the strength of the barrier holding you back. With all your attention on the power of the barrier, I want you now to come and get your goal.

[At first there is no movement. Then they slowly inch forward, eyes down, looking serious, even sad. She lets them struggle that way for a couple of minutes while the audience looks on. They don't even get half-way to the goal.]

"Okay that's enough. Thank you. Now I'd like you to go back to where you were again. We're going to turn it around. Think of something good in your life...

"it's probably going to last...

"Think of something bad in your life...

"and realize it's temporary, you'll get through it...

"Think of some success you've had...a time when you did something and you won or it came out right and you felt really pleased with yourself, proud of yourself...

"When you think about a new challenge, you can remember, 'Well, if I could do that, I can do this.'

"Think of all the strengths you have, talents that many other people don't have...

"There are quite a few once you start thinking about it...

"I've got a little gold star in my hand [it's a ceramic star glazed in a glossy golden color, about four inches tall]. I want you to focus your attention on it. Ignore the hands around your waist, and keep your eyes on

26

this star. Let the star represent what you could have. This star is your goal. Imagine the future, when you have achieved this goal...

"would you dress any different?

"Would you go places you now don't go?

"When you achieve this goal, what great things will you be saying to yourself?

"Think about the good things other people will say when you have this goal...

"What will it feel like to know you have attained this goal?

"What will it feel like to know you have what it took to achieve it?

"Barriers, please put your arms around them again.

"Now, you two: Keep your eyes on the goal. Do not take your eyes off this goal. Remember a time when you did very well at something...

"and I want you to know if you did very well once, you can do very well again...

"I want you to know a lot of people are behind you and want to help you...

"You will reach your goal!

"You have the strength. You have the talent. You have the determination.

"Keep your thoughts on this goal now. Stay aware of your feelings about this goal, and how you'll feel when you reach it. Now come get it! [Without hesitation, they both suddenly pull forward, smiling and laughing. The barriers are no match. The barriers unsuccessfully try to hold them back, but their effort is futile. In about three seconds, everyone is at the goal.

One of the people reaches up and touches the gold star with a big smile on his face. Everyone laughs.]

"Thank you. I'd like to ask the barriers a question: Did you notice anything different between the first time and the second time? [They both nod yes.] Okay, what was the difference? [One of them says, "He had more energy the second time." Klassy goes to the chalkboard and writes "energy".]

"Anything else you noticed? [One of them says, "She did it easier."] Klassy writes "easier" underneath "energy" on the board.]

"Anything else? [One says, "They were faster the second time." Klassy adds "faster" to the list.] I don't know if you in the audience could see their faces, but there were more smiles the second time. We'll assume smiles have to do with fun. [She adds "fun" to the list.] Okay, thanks to both of you. You two barriers can sit down.

[Klassy turns to the audience.] Now I'd like to ask you: What did you notice was different between the first time and the second time? [Somebody calls out, "More confidence the second time." Klassy adds "confidence" to the list. People say more things, and she adds them to the list: determination, strength, focus.]

[She turns to the two main participants in the demonstration — the goal seekers]: "Now I'd like to ask you, 'What was the difference for you?' [One of them says, "It reminded me of learning how to drive. When I first started, I focused my eyes on the front edge of the car, and I wasn't very effective. My Dad said over and over to look out ahead, and when I did, my driving got a lot better and I could relax." The other one says, "I felt stronger and more determined."]

"Thank you. That's a good one. Anything else you want to add? Okay, thank you for helping. You can sit down now."

What this demonstration shows very clearly, among other things, is that you are stronger, more determined, more powerful, and better able to get what you want when you stop focusing your attention on your obstacles and put your attention on your goal. That's the purpose of the question: *Does this help my goal?* If you want to be a photographer and get your business going, for example, it would help to continually ask this question. So when you have a little extra money and you're about it spend it on a weekend trip but it would really help your business to get a new lens, ask the question: Does this trip really help my goal? Does getting a lens really help my goal?

When someone tries to talk you into a job selling vacuum cleaners door-to-door, dangling riches before your eyes, this question will clarify the issue tremendously.

If there is one secret to success, this is it: Focus. You can't do it all. There just isn't enough time. You have to constantly choose one thing over another. How will you choose? By your feelings at the moment? By what you think others want? Or by how much it will help the most important goal you have?

"Obstacles," said Henry Ford, "are those frightful things you see when you take your eyes off the goal."

So ask yourself this question all the time, about everything. It will keep you focused on your goal, and this focus will give you power, speed, determination, strength, and fun.

What Does Life Expect From Me?

I borrowed this unusual question from Viktor Frankl. He had learned in his experience in Hitler's concentration camps that many of his fellow prisoners needed to change their attitude. Frankl wrote, "We had to learn ourselves and, furthermore, we had to teach the despairing men, that it did not really matter what we expected from life, but rather what life expected from us. We needed to stop asking about the meaning of life, and instead to think of ourselves as those who were being questioned by life — daily and hourly. Our answer must consist, not in talk and meditation, but in right action and in right conduct. Life ultimately means taking the responsibility to find the right answer to its problems and to fulfill the tasks which it constantly sets for each individual."

This is an interesting perspective, isn't it? Very different from our normal way of thinking. I think you might find it a productive question to ask yourself, "What task has life set for me?"

For example, Tom has seen his boss doing something unscrupulous, but he really wants his promotion, and he's the breadwinner of a growing family. He feels torn. It would give him a helpful perspective to ask, "What task is life setting for me here?"

Men in the concentration camp with Frankl sometimes tried to kill themselves. Because Frankl was a psychiatrist, life asked him to do something about it. He was called upon by his fellow prisoners to talk to the despairing men and find a way to renew their will to live.

Frankl learned the importance of finding meaning in life firsthand. When a person had some meaning — some reason to live — they were much less likely to kill themselves.

Frankl found that one man had a niece. The man was her only surviving family member. She needed him. So he had a reason to stay alive. There was a *meaning* to his suffering — a reason to endure. He needed to survive so he could look after that girl.

Another man had written several volumes of an important book series and it needed to be completed. He was the only person who could complete it. That was enough to keep him from committing suicide or just giving up and dying.

Frankl helped these men find something important life was asking them to do, and that was enough of a reason to live.

Viktor Frankl was a Jewish psychiatrist in Germany when Hitler took power and Frankl spent many years struggling to stay alive in concentration camps. During that time, he lost his wife, his brother, and both his parents — they either died in the camps or were sent to the gas ovens. He lost every possession he ever owned. Because he already knew a lot about psychology before he experienced these extreme circumstances, his observations have an extraordinary depth that makes his slim book, *Man's Search for Meaning*, very much worth reading. His perspective on finding meaning in life is different from any other I have encountered. He wrote, for example:

> "The meaning of life differs from person to person, from day to day and from hour to hour. What matters, therefore, is not the meaning of life in general but rather the specific meaning of a person's life at a given moment. To put the question in general terms would be comparable to the question posed to a chess champion, "Tell me, Master, what is the best move in the world?" There simply is no such thing as the best or even a good move apart from a particular situation in a game and the particular personality of one's opponent. The same holds true for human existence. One should not search for an abstract meaning of life. Everyone has his own specific vocation or mission in life to carry out a concrete assignment which demands fulfillment."

I love that line: "...to carry out a concrete assignment which demands fulfillment." For example, Frankl tried to keep his fellow prisoners from committing suicide. The Nazis had made it strictly forbidden to stop a fellow prisoner from killing himself. If you cut down a prisoner in the process of hanging himself, you (and probably everyone in your bunkhouse) would be severely punished. So Frankl had to catch people before they actually attempted suicide. This, he felt, was a concrete assignment which demanded fulfillment. He was a psychiatrist. He was the most qualified prisoner in his camp to fulfill this assignment.

The men would often confide in Frankl, since he was a psychiatrist. The two men I mentioned above had told Frankl they had decided to commit suicide. Both of them had basically the same reason: They had nothing more to expect from life. All they could expect was endless suffering, starvation, torture, heartbreak, and in the end, probably the gas chamber.

"In both cases," wrote Frankl, "it was a question of getting them to realize that life was still expecting something from them..." After talking with the men, Frankl discovered one of them was a scientist who had written several volumes of a book, but the project was incomplete. The other man had a niece in another country, and he was her last living relative.

These are concrete answers to the question, "What does life expect from me?" The first man needed to finish his work. The other needed to find his niece and take care of her. Frankl had done nothing more than help them see they had a concrete assignment they had not yet fulfilled.

Even for people in less desperate situations than a concentration camp, a sense of purposelessness can produce fatigue, depression, alcoholism, and suicide. A lack of purpose creates all kinds of mental and emotional ill-health. And even if the ill-health wasn't *created* by purposelessness, finding a purpose can often cure the health problem.

It doesn't matter what other factors are doing well — money, family, kids, work, health — without a sense of purpose, those things won't make you happy, and psychological problems will tend to plague you.

And you can't "make something up" just to have a purpose. Any random goal is not good enough. It's got to be real for you. It has to have meaning for you. This is not a quick and easy fix. This is a profound and fundamental question: What concrete assignment do you really feel is demanding fulfillment?

Each person's life is unique. The concrete assignment a person needs to fulfill is different for every person, and different for each person at different times under different circumstances. Frankl discovered that a prisoner would not commit suicide once he realized his unique obligation to life.

Frankl's observations have been borne out by recent research. Investigators at New York State Psychiatric Institute studied eighty-four people suffering major depression trying to determine why thirty-nine of them had never attempted to kill themselves. Instead of asking what makes depressed people want to die, they asked what makes them want to live.

The study revealed that age, sex, religious persuasion or education level did not predict who would attempt suicide. But strong reasons to live did predict it rather well. The depressed patients who responded on the questionnaire with *more reasons for living* showed less hopelessness and were less likely to try to kill themselves.

Other studies have shown that students who feel they have some purpose in life are far less likely to get involved with drugs.

Purpose in life. Meaning in life. These are not superfluous issues reserved for philosophy classes. Frankl's question brings us to the heart of a vital matter. The question makes us look at our situation from an unusual point of view.

Thinking about "what you want out of life" is a common thing to do; it is looking at your situation in a common way. But what about asking what life wants out of you? Not that you should ignore what you want out of life. I don't think these two points of view are entirely opposing, and in fact, I would add to Frankl's view that the ideal purpose fulfills both. For both of the prisoners who had decided to commit suicide, Frankl's point of view helped them find their purpose, but for both of them, the purpose was not merely a duty. It was also something they wanted very strongly and had simply forgotten about or given up on. For each man, their purpose was something they desired and also something *they* felt was a concrete assignment that demanded fulfillment.

Frankl's question is worth asking — especially if your aim doesn't seem very clear to you. By looking at your life from another angle, you can sometimes see what you've disregarded or overlooked. What needs to be done and what you strongly want to do is often staring you in the face without you seeing it.

For Michael W. Fox, his concrete assignment was unmistakable. Fox is now a veterinarian and author of several books. When he was nine years old, he was walking home from school when he looked through a fence and saw a ghastly sight: A large trash bin overflowing with dead dogs and cats. He was looking into the backyard of a veterinary clinic. "I never knew the reason for this mass extermination," Fox said, "but I was, from that time on, committed to doing all I could to help animals, deciding at age nine that I had to be a veterinarian."

Here was a concrete assignment life had presented to Fox. He saw something that needed to be done, and he strongly wanted to do something about it. He became a veterinarian and has been reducing the suffering of animals ever since. He has worked to educate people and pass legislation that reflects more respect for all animals.

A clear aim can convert a feeling of horror into a resolve to do something about it. A clear aim can transform a feeling of despair into grim determination. If there is anything in your life you feel you've given up on, or if you feel despair or hopelessness about something, this is your wake up call. A clear aim can change a self-defeating, counterproductive emotion into a constructive feeling that leads to constructive action. For example, during the Korean War, the Chinese government tried to brainwash captured U.S. soldiers. The Chinese used every technique they could think of to make the POWs give up their belief in personal freedom and take up a belief in the greatness of communism.

The captives were tortured, starved, and psychologically assaulted — unless they converted. In one of the prison camps, three-fourths of the POWs had died, and things looked pretty bleak to those still alive. They were feeling demoralized and hopeless. Not only did their chances for survival look slim, but they would have to endure terrible suffering until the end. The POWs were beginning to give up on life.

Then one man said, "We've got to stay alive, we've got to let others know about the horrors of Communism. We've got to live to bring back the armies and fight these evil people. Communism must not win!"

This was a turning point for every American in that prison because their meaningless suffering was transformed into a mission. Their despair was turned into resolve. Their feeling of hopelessness was converted into firm determination. And from that point, prisoners stopped dying. They made it back to the U.S. They lived to tell the world what happened.

A single definite, worthwhile, heartfelt purpose can transform a horrible experience into a sacred calling, crusade, a holy aspiration, a true mission. I've read about and I've had personal experience with the same transformation many times.

Viktor Frankl wrote, "Any attempt to restore a man's inner strength in the camp had first to succeed in showing him some future goal...Woe to him who saw no more sense in his life, no aim, no purpose, and therefore no point in carrying on. He was soon lost."

The psychologist, Abraham Maslow, studied exceptional people to find out what unusually healthy people were like. Until Maslow came along, psychologists mostly studied mentally ill people to find out why they were ill and how they became that way. Maslow felt we could also learn something from the study of fulfilled, happy, successful people. That became his life's work. And one of the things he found out about these "self-actualized" people was that "every one of them, without exception, were devoted to a cause outside their own skin."

They were devoted to a cause. They had a clear aim. And for these exceptional people, it was a clear aim beyond satisfying their personal needs. They were working on a concrete assignment that demanded fulfillment.

If you want to join the ranks of the self-actualized, get yourself a purpose that fires you up. Find something that you think is needed, that you feel is important, that you want very strongly to see accomplished. If you don't have one, I have one for you. I've thought long and hard about what is needed in this world, and here it is: We must win the war against pessimism, cynicism, and defeatism, and you can help. You can take up this banner and put your powers to the test.

Maybe you already have a clear aim. Or maybe your clear aim is not so global in scope. If not, don't sweat it. But don't try to accomplish a clear aim if your heart isn't in it. Pick something important to you. Choose something that fits your situation. Remember the man who had a niece to take care of.

But don't choose a goal beneath you, either. Defeatism reveals itself in the setting of low goals — goals too small or petty — goals below your capabilities. Setting a low or petty goal is a kind of preemptive defeat. You've given up on bigger goals before you've even tried. For someone with no purpose at all or in a very restricted situation (like a concentration camp), a small goal is all you may be able to realistically consider. But as your level of psychological fitness increases (and/or as your material conditions improve), there comes a time when an all-in crusade is called for as a context for your life.

There isn't one right purpose which you must find and follow. Delete that kind of magical thinking from your thoughts forever! Any constructive purpose is better than no purpose and some are better than others. Some are good for now, but no good if pursued too long. The important thing is that you like your purpose and feel it is important.

We don't know if life really does expect anything from us. But asking that question calls forth deep personal answers of meaning and purpose. Try pondering the question for a few days and you'll see what I mean.

How Can I Prevent This From Ever Happening Again?

Here is a useful approach to the inevitable misfortunes that will come your way. It is a way to resolve your negative feelings and use the misfortune in a practical way. When something unfortunate happens, you will naturally have it on your mind for some time. You'll think about it. Often you will merely remember it and feel bad. If you caused it, you might feel guilty. If you didn't cause it, you might ruminate on how you wish it hadn't happened, or how upset you are at what the consequences will be. As long as your mind is on it, you might as well take advantage of it and see if something useful can be gained by pondering it. The most direct way to do that is to ponder the question, "What could I do to prevent that from happening to me again?"

This is a way to direct your mind. You're already thinking about it, but the way most people naturally think about misfortunes does not help. This question goes along with the impetus of your mind, but aims that impetus in a more productive direction.

After thinking about it you may conclude nothing you can do will prevent it from happening again, in which case, you can ponder what would be the best way to respond to it next time, or what you will do now to minimize the consequences.

Pondering these questions will satisfy your mind's desire to think about it, will minimize how bad it makes you feel, and will help you learn something useful for the future.

What is the Best Use of My Time Right Now?

This is Alan Lakein's question. Lakein is the author of the famous book, *How to Get Control of Your Time and Your Life*, and he's the original expert on time management. This question is a good one for almost any situation. It can clarify your mind in moments and get you back on track. Lakein recommends asking it several times a day. First you need to know what your goals are. Then you can ask the question to your heart's content. The way you use your time is and always will be an extremely important question. All you have is time, and what you have is limited. I know, I know, you've heard it all before, but you can't hear it enough because it is human nature to take it all for granted, act as if we've got all the time in the world, "fritter and waste the hours in an offhand way" on stuff that isn't important at all, and then be shocked and horrified when we suddenly realize ten years have gone by and we haven't accomplished nearly what we wanted to. No one told you when to run. You missed the starting gun.

As the Pink Floyd song says: "The sun is the same in a relative way, but you're older. Shorter of breath, one day closer to death." Not the sort of thing we normally like to think about, but time is running out for all of us. Courageously facing that fact head-on can really improve your motivation to use your time better. Lakein's question can help.

Ask the question. Several times a day. And think about it. This is one question that deserves some time.

How Can I Use This to Accomplish My Goal?

When I first started speaking in public to promote my book, I got pretty nervous. I had never done much public speaking before. I tried many things to deal with it, but the one that worked the best was *using* the nervousness to help me accomplish my goal.

Originally, I decided that each adrenaline jolt would be my cue to go over the speech outline in my head. That worked pretty well. I stopped dreading the nervousness and stopped trying to avoid having it. An adrenaline rush became a welcome opportunity to make sure I knew exactly what I was going to say. This directly countered my main fear — that I would lose my train of thought in front of the group.

I got the general principle: To *use* the feeling of anxiety to remind me of something. I tried out several things. The one that worked best was saying to myself, "I will *make* them get how important this is." That's what I wanted to go through my head as I stood in front of an audience. I practiced that thought over and over whenever I experienced an adrenaline rush.

And while I practiced saying this to myself, I imagined saying it to myself while looking at the audience, so the audience became associated with that thought — the audience itself became a trigger for that statement or thought.

I came up with this after doing a few speeches. I noticed the audience listened with the attitude, "this is interesting." But I wanted them to sit up and pay attention to what I was saying — as if it could help them or someone they loved, as if it would make a difference, *as if it were important!* I wanted to have a real impact on them. I wanted their lives to be forever better. I didn't want them to listen to me as a mere form of entertainment. This was something I really wanted. It was a sincere, heartfelt desire. And that was the key.

So every time I got a jolt, I would say to myself, "I will *make* them get how important this is!" And thanks to the jolt, I said it with extra intensity.

In other words, I used something that seemingly was against my goal, and I used it in service to my goal.

Whatever happens that seems to directly hinder you goal, try this question on it. Ask how you can use your barrier to help you with your goal.

For example, let's say a man has a goal to become a manager. He works as a clerk. He works a forty hour week. That's forty hours of not being able to write resumes, take training, or in any way move forward toward his goal. True or false?

He asks himself this question. He is working as a clerk, and he thinks of that as a barrier. So he asks how he can use working-as-a-clerk to help him accomplish his goal. For several days he asks this question and so far hasn't come up with any good answers. But then today he realizes that he interacts with his manager occasionally throughout the day.

"Maybe I could see what he's doing right and what I would do differently if I were manager," he decides. That's a good idea. Then he realizes that as a clerk he deals with people all the time. Maybe he could improve his general ability to deal with people and that would help him become a better manager.

And now he's on a roll. He realizes that he casually talks with people all the time. Maybe he might find out about management opportunities.

Maybe he could talk to his manager about managing, asking him, for example, if he had it to do over again, is there anything he would study before he started managing?

He is limited in what he can do while he is at work because he has to do his clerking job. But he could find leads, come up with ideas, and so on that he could pursue on his off-hours. And when he gets home he could make notes, keeping a notebook on what he saw that worked and didn't work about what his manager did.

He could make notes of what it is like as an employee to be on the receiving end of the way his manager deals with him, and that could help him in the future when he's a manager and has a manager's point of view and starts to forget the employee's point of view, etc.

The point of this question is to get you thinking. When something seems to be interfering with your goal, ask yourself if you can somehow use it to *help* your goal. Sometimes you will come up with brilliant ideas.

What's Good About This?

The compass (and its use in navigation) was developed in the Mediterranean because the sailors there had several disadvantages: very deep water, winds that varied a lot in the winter, and skies that were usually overcast. So you couldn't reliably navigate by sounding, by the wind, or by the stars. Those were the three ways sailors all over the world used to navigate. In the Indian oceans, the monsoon winds are so regular (they change directions with the seasons) you could easily determine your direction by simply noticing which way the wind was blowing. And they have clear tropical skies so they could usually navigate by the stars.

Northern Europe is on the continental shelves of the Atlantic, so the water is shallow enough that sailors could drop a lead weight attached to a rope to the sea floor to find their depth, and thus could tell where they were by how deep the water was. This was called making a sounding, and it was a very accurate method of locating one's position in charted waters.

But the sailors of the Mediterranean had to develop some way to navigate without shallow waters, clear skies or predictable winds. And because they had to develop navigation by compass, Spain, which borders both the Atlantic and the Mediterranean, was the first to find and colonize the New World.

Without having the know-how to navigate by compass, nobody in their right mind would have sailed across the Atlantic. There would have been no guarantee they'd be able to find their way back. They'd have no familiar landmarks, no soundings would work, wind directions would of course be unknown, and whether or not they'd have clear skies was unknown.

The "disadvantage" of sailing the Mediterranean turned out to be quite an advantage for Spain.

But of course, given the mind's natural negative bias, I'm sure most people of Spain assumed their sailing conditions were only a disadvantage.

The lesson here is simple: When you think something is a disadvantage, think again. Assume there will be an advantage in it and then find it or make it. This intention is a fundamental key to a good attitude. With it, the inevitable setbacks in life won't bring you down as much and you will handle problems more effectively.

I know some people would scoff at this idea. It's too airy-fairy. It might remind them of some annoyingly positive people they know to whom everything is great, but somehow, behind their forced smile, you can see it's all a facade.

But this idea can be used with depth, rather than as a way to merely show a pleasant face to the world or hide your pain from yourself. It can be done with intelligence and wisdom.

Many people think cynicism and pessimism are good in some ways. But they aren't good. Negative attitudes are actually dangerous, unhealthy, damaging, and contagious.

In a study at Washington University in St. Louis, researchers interviewed people who had experienced a either a plane crash, a tornado, or a mass shooting. They interviewed the survivors a few weeks after the traumatic event and then again three years later.

In the first interview, some people said something good came out of the event. Some reported they realized life was too short not to pursue their most important goals, or they realized how important their family was to them. Three years later, those were the people who recovered from the trauma most successfully.

In an interview in *Psychology Today*, Carl Sagan said of his fight with cancer, "This is my third time having to deal with intimations of mortality. And every time it's a character-building experience. You get a much clearer perspective on what's important and what isn't, the preciousness and beauty of life...I would recommend almost dying to everybody. I think it's a really good experience."

Think now about something you have that you normally consider a disadvantage...

Are you in debt? Did you have a rough childhood? Were you poor? Didn't have the advantages wealthier kids had? Do you lack education? Do you have a bad habit? Has something terrible happened to you? Are you frustrated with your career? Not making as much progress as you'd like? Feel stagnant?

Pick one thing in your life you normally think is a bad thing.

Now ask yourself, "What's good about it?" Or if there is really nothing outright good about it, how could you *make* something good about it?

If you don't get a good answer right away, that only means it's a tough question. And it means when you find a good answer, it will probably make a bigger difference. Try living with the question for several weeks or even months. Ponder it while you drive. Wonder about it while you shower. Ask yourself the question every time you eat breakfast. Live with the question and you will get answers.

And your answers will help you make things turn out better for you. As Klassy often says, "Things turn out best for those who make the best of how things turn out." As I write this, Klassy is at her ill mother's house, taking care of her, and I only see her on week-ends, and not even every weekend. I miss her terribly. Obviously this is a bad thing.

But I'm using this time to work on a book. Instead of moping or simply suffering, I am making the most of it, taking advantage of it. When the ordeal is over, we will have gained a lot from this misfortune. That was my commitment when it started and by thought and action I'm making it come true.

It is not putting your head in the clouds to take advantage of your reality — what you have, where you are, and when you are. It's an entirely practical way to deal with "disadvantages."

If you have a tendency to simply feel bad about your disadvantages, even *that* can become an advantage. Trying to overcome your tendency might teach you something valuable — something you couldn't have learned without it. And you can teach what you learned to your children, which could make a difference to the whole trajectory of their lives.

Trying to make the best of something that has already happened helps create solutions. It helps make things better. It is even better for your health. It keeps you from feeling as bad when bad stuff happens. It lowers your stress, and less stress is good for you. As Richard H. Hoffmann, MD, said:

> The human body is a delicately adjusted mechanism. Whenever its even tenor is startled by some intruding emotion like sudden fright, anger or worry, the sympathetic nervous system flashes an emergency signal and the organs and glands spring into action. The adrenal glands shoot into the blood stream a surcharge of adrenaline which raises the blood sugar above normal needs. The pancreas then secretes insulin to burn the excess fuel. But this bonfire burns not only the excess but the normal supply. The result is a blood sugar shortage and an underfeeding of the vital organs. So the adrenals supply another charge,

the pancreas burns the fuel again, and the vicious cycle goes on. This battle of the glands brings on exhaustion.

Frequent negative emotions play havoc on your system. The idea that something good may come from your misfortune allows you to consider that things might not be as bad as they seem at the moment, and in a sense, makes it possible to procrastinate feeling bad. Procrastinate long enough, and you might just skip it altogether. This makes for less stress and better health.

Volunteers at the Common Cold Research Unit in England filled out a questionnaire. The researcher, Sheldon Cohen, discovered that the more positive the volunteers' attitudes were, the less likely they were to catch a cold. And even when they did catch a cold, the more positive their attitude was, the more mild their symptoms were.

IT WORKS IN BUSINESS TOO

W. Clement Stone became rich selling insurance and then running an insurance company. In one of Stone's books, he wrote that whenever someone came to him with a problem, he would always say, "That's good!" This puzzled people sometimes. They might be one of his salespeople talking about a serious problem — a problem that cost Stone's company a lot of money —

and Stone would answer back with enthusiasm: "That's good!"

Years ago when I first read this, I thought it was over the top. Too much. But I've thought a lot about it over the years and I've tried it, and I've decided that maybe there are some things that sound stupid but are really smart.

When anything happens, usually some aspects of it are an advantage and some aspects are a disadvantage. For example, when you buy a new car, it will probably need less repair work than an older car. That's one advantage. Maybe it gets better gas mileage. There's another advantage. But it is more likely to get stolen. That's a disadvantage. And your insurance payments are higher. You get the idea. The point is, almost any event has both good and bad aspects to it.

When you first hear about a problem, your first reaction is probably to see only the disadvantages. This is a natural reaction. You focus all your attention on the bad aspects of the event. This puts you in a bad mood — a state of mind not only unpleasant as an experience, but also one that makes you less effective at dealing with the problem. If you react like this to unexpected or unfortunate events often or habitually, it will cause extra stress, so it's bad for your health. The habit would be a good thing to change. I suggest trying Stone's method. It will take some practice, but it can eventually become a habit.

When a problem lands in your lap, say, "That's good!" (Note: Don't necessarily say it out loud. It will make some people mad.) And then immediately start doing two things:

1) look for the advantages that might be wrapped up in this "problem" (which may be difficult at first), and

2) look to see how you can turn it to your advantage, and take steps to make it so.

This approach will make you more effective. You can plainly see why. You don't waste any time bemoaning what already exists, and your thoughts turn immediately to how you can turn it to your advantage. No suffering is endured getting into a worse mood than is absolutely necessary. Your attitude toward the circumstances is open.

Your point of view — whatever it may be — is not something fixed or permanent. It can be changed fairly easily. And when you change the way you think about something, it changes the way you feel about it. And when you change the way you feel about it, your actions change too — in this case, for the better. Try it.

And remember, if you have trouble at first learning to do this, that's good!

THE ORIGINAL MISTAKEN ASSUMPTION

The people of Japan and Germany were defeated in World War Two. Many of them probably thought this was a bad thing. But aren't the majority of the people in those countries far better off than they would have been if they had *won* the war? Wasn't that really the best thing that could have happened to the majority of the ordinary citizens?

At the time, however, they didn't know that. And I'm sure many of them were very distressed about this "bad" turn of events.

Haven't you had a similar experience? Something happened you thought at first was terrible and you got upset about it, but later you were really glad it happened? If you can think of a time when this happened to you, keep that memory in your mind whenever something bad happens.

You don't know what the future holds. The new "bad" event might be good. I'm not talking about fooling yourself. You're making an assumption anyway. You really don't know if this might turn out to your advantage. You might as well assume it will be, and start making it so.

A mistake might not be a mistake. You might think that you should have done this or shouldn't have done that. But it would be better to ask what advantages your already-done deeds give you and exploit them in the present.

The architect Bonano erected a freestanding bell tower for a cathedral, but he built it on soft subsoil — a bad mistake which made the tower lean over. That mistake created a large tourist industry and put the town on the map. People came from all over the world to see the leaning tower of Pisa. Galileo conducted his famous gravity experiments from that tower *because* it was leaning.

Of course, an historical example is all fine and well, but what about you? Don't you have things in your life right now you consider a disadvantage? Aren't there conditions you "know" are bad? That you wish would go away?

Choose one right now and suspend your negative judgment about it for a moment and ponder this question: Is it possible your disadvantage is an advantage in disguise? Or could you *make* an advantage out of it?

If you don't want to ponder this for weeks, you can do a little concentrated pondering. Write this question at the top of a piece of paper, "What is good about this?" And force yourself to come up with 15 answers and write them down.

Then take another piece of paper. At the top write, "How could I *turn* this into an advantage?" Make yourself come up with 15 more answers.

At the end of this exercise, which will only take you an hour or two, your perspective on the "problem" will be totally altered. The "problem" will have lost most of its power to bring you down. This process can undemoralize you. It can restore lost motivation. It can give you strength and effectiveness and even good feelings.

UNWANTED AND UNLOVED

Irwin Kahn wrote to Dear Abby. When he was ten years old, Irwin's mother sent him to a children's home. He was very hurt by this. She kept Irwin's younger brother and sister, but got rid of him. Ouch! His mom said Irwin was too much of a troublemaker.

He was an emotional mess for a while and developed a severe stuttering problem. But he was assigned a "Big Brother" and the staff of the children's home were good people, and this combination helped him develop some inner strength and a sense of values.

At age seventeen, he left the home to make his way in the world. "I educated myself," he said, "overcame my stuttering, became a successful corporate CEO, and now enjoy multimillionaire status. I retired at 52."

If you think about it, what seemed a terrible disadvantage — being unwanted and unloved — might have been an advantage in disguise. This conclusion seems so much the opposite of what anyone would normally think. But the fact is, he came into the care of people who were devoting their lives to helping others. He came under the influence of a Big Brother who voluntarily and out of genuine kindness spent his time to help a young person. If he hadn't been rejected by his mother, Irwin would not have met these people or been influenced by them. Instead, he would have been raised by a mother who clearly didn't care about him.

We've got to face the facts: Our natural negative bias makes us automatically reject certain kinds of events, but depending on your attitude, those events could really and truly turn out to contain a hidden advantage which you will only see if you look.

When the energy crisis engulfed the world in the 1970s, Brazil was hurt badly. Oil imports were taking half the available foreign currency, and the country was heavily in debt. But because of the crisis, Brazilians looked elsewhere for fuel. They had to look no further than their own backyard.

One of the things Brazil had was a huge sugar cane crop. So they used it to make alcohol, and started using alcohol as fuel. Today, 90% of cars sold in Brazil run on alcohol, which burns much more cleanly than gas. Almost all the cars sold in Brazil can burn gasoline and ethanol equally well, and most fuel stations sell both. To this day, Brazil is the only country in the world with true fuel competition. It has helped their economy tremendously, especially when oil prices have spiked (something that seriously hurts the rest of the world because there is no widely available alternative fuel that most of the cars can use). Brazil just passed Britain to become the sixth largest economy in the world.

They found advantages in their disadvantage. Because alcohol became their chief fuel, air quality in their cities improved.

The sugar cane is ground to a pulp, and the juice is extracted and fermented. So they had hundreds of thousands of tons of juiceless pulp. They had to pay garbage collectors to take it away.

But you and I have to drill it into our noggins that a disadvantage (like tons of pulp) may be an advantage in disguise if we think that way. Brazilians did. And they found things to do with the pulp. They burn the pulp to generate electricity, relieving the necessity of building new dams on the Amazon river — dams that cause flooding and environmental damage. And burning the pulp adds no permanent carbon dioxide into the atmosphere, because the growing plants absorb as much as is released in the burning.

The pulp is also made into a nutritious feed for cattle.

It is an old positive-thinking maxim that "trouble brings the seeds of good fortune." It may one of those ideas that makes itself true. If you think you can make an advantage out of a disadvantage, you may try, and if you try, you greatly increase the odds of it happening.

But if you close your mind to the situation — if you make up your mind it is just bad — you are less likely to think of a way to turn it to your advantage.

You have something to gain and nothing to lose by taking this idea — that trouble contains the seeds of good fortune — and burning it into your mind. Make it an automatic part of your thinking. Practice asking the question, "What's good about this?" Make the question come to mind naturally and easily. Have it so ingrained that it is your first thought when trouble comes your way. It will give you power to overcome difficulties and prevent life from sinking you into the quicksand of despair. It will give you a path to better future.

When Henry Ford was running the Ford Motor Company, he had to overcome one problem after another (just like the rest of us). He was exceptionally good at turning problems into opportunities. For example, on their lunch hour some of his employees used the scrap wood left over from making dashboards and burned it as firewood. They cooked their lunches with it.

The problem was all the charcoal left over. It was starting to accumulate. Ford needed to get rid of it. But how?

His first idea was to make his dealers take it. He said for every train carload of his cars they bought, they had to take a carload of charred wood with it. How they disposed of it would be their problem. As you can guess, this didn't go over very well with the dealers.

Eventually, Ford's "problem" was solved — in a very profitable way. A friend of Ford's, Mr. E.G. Kingsford, bought the charcoal and packaged it with a little grill and some lighter fluid and sold it in supermarkets. Kingsford briquettes have been earning a healthy profit ever since.

By thinking about it, a problem became an opportunity in disguise. Ford actually profited from his "problem."

The actor Edward James Olmos grew up in East L.A. and his parents divorced when he was seven. He lived with ten other people in a three-room house (including the kitchen) with a dirt floor. Growing up this way is obviously a disadvantage, right? Olmos sees it differently, and that's why he is successful. He said, "Some people say they didn't have a choice. They're poor or brown or crippled. They had no parents. Well, you can use any one of those excuses to keep your life from growing. Or you can say, 'Okay, this is where I am, but I'm not going to let it stop me. Instead, I'm gonna turn it around and make it my strength.' That's what I did."

Sometimes there is a blessing to trouble without any intention to make it that way. You might get in a fender-bender and the cop who shows up asks you out on a date and you end up marrying.

But often, when something bad happens, it's just bad, or at least it seems that way. There doesn't seem to be anything redeeming about it. And since we're usually in a negative state of mind when trouble strikes, we're in no mood to try to find anything redeeming about it!

Here's the problem with that: Your mind will tend to see what you expect to see, unless you have strong and clear evidence to the contrary.

If you see the "bad" event as bad, you are not likely to get any clear evidence you're wrong. It happens sometimes, but not very often. Since there is no obvious reality to confirm or contradict your opinion, your mind is free to see what's bad about the situation, and equally free to ignore what might be good about it. And that's exactly what your mind will do if you don't do anything to stop it.

And by seeing what's bad, sometimes you can actually make the situation worse. If you think it's bad and you throw in the towel, you might miss what you could have done to solve the problem, or even turn it to your advantage. And by not doing anything, sometimes the problem can get worse.

This question, "What's good about this?" makes you open your eyes and see what opportunities you might be able to cultivate. It turns your attention to the future, to doing something about it. It changes your attitude from one of avoidance and rejection to one of acceptance and alertness. It puts you in a better frame of mind for dealing with the "trouble."

When something "bad" happens, you can accept that it's bad, or you can try to concentrate on what is good about it, or you can make something good out of it.

Am I beating this to death? Maybe so. But then tomorrow when someone doesn't call you back or you burn your dinner or you see your child's report card and it's bad, how will you react?

If you take this idea and make it an ingrained part of your thinking, you can take many of the circumstances that in the past would have just been unfortunate, and you can change them into something that creates benefits for you and the people around you. And maybe for the world at large. At the very least, it will change your attitude for the better.

There are some things that "everyone knows" are bad: a home burned to the ground, a divorce, a lost job, a sick child, and there are millions of smaller inconveniences that if you asked 100 people, 99 of them would all agree that yes, those are definitely bad and there is nothing good about them. But what everyone agrees about isn't necessarily true.

DO NOT STOP YOURSELF

You may already know that "assuming the worst" is bad for your life, but maybe you don't know how to stop yourself from doing it. The negative assumptions come automatically and once you think that way, it's difficult to make the thoughts go away.

But now you have a way to do it. Don't try to stop thinking anything. Trying *not* to think something negative makes you fixate on the negative. There is a better way.

Simply ask yourself the question, "What's good about this?" Or even, "What *might* be good about this?" And keep asking it over and over. Not forcing. Not with any frustration. Not trying to stop yourself from thinking anything else. Just calmly repeat that question to yourself. Keep looking at your life through this question. Ponder it.

Keep doing that when troubles big and small come your way and after awhile — a month, a year — you'll start thinking that way automatically. You will start to trust it. It will become a natural part of your thinking. Trouble will happen and you'll automatically and naturally start wondering what is good about it or how you can turn it to your advantage.

Can you imagine what that will do to your calm during a crisis? Can you imagine how much better you will be at keeping your wits about you?

Ask the question. All by itself, it can transform the quality of your experience, and through the change in your experience, it will change your attitude, your expressions, your behavior, alter the actions you take, and through those, actually change the world you live in, and it will benefit others. When something "bad" happens, ask the question, "What's good about this?"

What is My Goal Here?

Even if you have a goal, it is abstract, no matter how concretely you have defined it, because you can only really take action on it in this very moment. So it's an excellent practice to try to keep in mind one clear goal for what you're doing now. To know your goal at this moment. Asking the question, "What is my goal here?" — and doing it often — helps you keep your goals in mind, and it can be illuminating.

When you ask the question, sometimes you just drop what you're doing because it is not a goal you want to pursue now that you think about it. For example, if you are busy criticizing someone, ask yourself, "What is my goal here?" You may find what you are trying to accomplish is to make the other person feel bad, or punish them for something they did. This goal might have been created without your consent by an automatic, emotional reaction. In other words, you didn't really consciously or deliberately choose that goal.

But now that you've asked the question, "What is my goal here?" you can choose. You can think about what you really want in this situation. Let's say you decide what you really want is to make sure the person doesn't do it again. Then you'd have a clear goal and a clear path for action. You might simply decide to say to the person, "Please don't do that again." Or, "If you do that again, you're fired."

Ask yourself, "What is my goal here?" Ask it all the time. It will help you accomplish your goals faster. It's effective. It's therapeutic. It's healthy. And it will make you more productive. You'll waste less of your time doing things you really wouldn't do if you thought about it.

Wants are fleeting, changing, whimsical, and often conflicting — and are sometimes too short-term and motivated by immediate gratification. For this reason, "What do I want?" is a lousy question. "What is my goal here?" is much better.

A bad attitude is often just insufficient purposefulness. When you're on track, thinking about your goal and moving toward your goal, you're not bothered by annoyances because it is counterproductive to even think about it, just as when you're pulling your son out of the way of a speeding car, it would be irrelevant whether or not he was sassing you. Don't resist your feelings or fight them. Just get back on purpose.

Pondering how you can accomplish your goal keeps your mind on your goal, and that's one of the best things to keep your mind on. Make your goal the central organizing principle of your life. You can do that with this question, asked many times a day, every day, like an obsession.

Ask yourself, "What is my goal here?" Ask it all the time. You'll feel better and get more of what you want.

What is Another Way to Look at This?

The best way to direct your mind is with a question. You can make up your own question to ponder or you can take one of the questions I've come up with and found to be productive. This one is almost universally helpful: When you feel bothered by something, ask yourself, "What is another way to look at this?"

You look at your situation in a certain way, and it is automatic. You generally don't take the time to think about the *best* way to look at the events in your life. The events happen, and you interpret them however you normally interpret those kinds of events, influenced by whatever mood you happen to be in at the moment.

But whatever interpretation you make of a particular event isn't the only one possible. And if the way you interpret it doesn't help you deal with it, it's a good time to explore other ways to look at it.

How would your grandmother have looked at the same circumstance? How would the person you most admire look at it? How would you have looked at this when you were ten years old? These are all questions to help you get outside your point of view and look at the situation from a different angle.

If you feel bad or you're not getting things done, or you've got a problem you can't seem to figure out, it pays to take another look at the thing. You've looked at it from your automatic perspective already. So get outside your own point of view and see what you see.

One way to get outside your own point of view is to literally imagine yourself not looking out of your own eyes. For example, imagine being Mother Theresa sitting across from you as you tell her your situation. Imagine that you are Mother Theresa listening to you.

Look at yourself over there. How would you (as Mother Theresa) view this person's (your) problem? How would you look at it if you were Mother Theresa or Gandhi or Lincoln?

And don't try to be yourself asking how Mother Theresa would look at it, but try to imagine yourself as her, and you as a stranger and really see how she would see you. Give yourself advice from Mother Theresa's point of view (or whoever you chose). This is a very simple way to "think outside the box."

This is not that hard to do. It is almost like daydreaming. But it will help you tremendously if you feel stuck. It will help you change the way you feel about a situation, and help you deal with it better. You will gain more flexibility in your point of view and you won't get so stuck in a single perspective that may be counterproductive.

Think of something you feel stuck with right now. Something that bothers you. Or something that makes you feel bad when you think about it. Choose one thing.

Now ask this question: What is another way to look at this? Keep pondering the question for several days. On your way to work, turn off the radio and ponder the question. While you're in the shower, ponder the question. As you are lying in bed ready to go to sleep, ponder the question.

When you think of an answer that seems surprising and illuminating, write it down and then keep asking the question. Maybe you can think of something even better. There is always still another way to look at the same situation. Pondering this question is a good way to find it.

What Else?

This is a question from my book, *Principles For Personal Growth*. It's good question for a lot of situations. For example, Yale psychologist Alan Kazdin did an experiment with kids suffering from "conduct disorder" — young people prone to violence, vandalism, truancy, and hostility.

Psychologists have tried many different things over the years to try to curb this disorder, but not very much has been successful. How do you change a problem child into a healthy, happy, productive youngster? Theories abound. Results are rare.

So Kazdin tried something unusual. He taught the troublemaking kids and their parents how to think up options for handling situations, and to come up with different ways of interpreting situations — other ways besides using hostility.

The result: Significantly less troublemaking. Fewer problems. It worked.

The question is, "*Why* did it work?" Think about it for a moment. When the only response you have is hostility, that's what you do, regardless of whether it gets you the results you're after. Kazdin trained these people essentially to ask themselves, "What else?" The parents and their kids learned to say to themselves before they responded to something, "Okay, I could do that (what I've always done), but what *else* could I do?" He taught them to think of new options they'd never thought of before.

And also he taught them to ask, "What else could it *mean*?" When someone bumped into one of these kids, for example, instead of immediately interpreting it as a hostile attack or a threat, he learned to ask himself, "Okay, it *might* mean that, but what *else* could it mean?"

It seems such a simple solution to a difficult problem. But it's harder than you might think. Our minds naturally streamline our mental processes. Asking "What else?" makes the decision-process more complex. So it takes some deliberate effort to turn your mind to the task of coming up with alternative ideas. It isn't really difficult, but it doesn't come naturally.

This question is useful in many different ways. As I'm writing this, it's really cold outside, and even though a little while ago I had the heater turned up and my feet covered, my feet were still as cold as ice. Turning the heater up and covering my feet were obvious solutions. But, I asked myself *what else* might work? What else could I do?

When you ask yourself a question, it awakens a part of your brain that answers questions. Ask a question, and your mind seems to search through all the things you've heard or know, and it often comes up with something.

I suddenly remembered something Klassy told me years ago: "If your hands are cold, cover your head." She used to live in Lake Tahoe, California, and she learned how to deal with very cold weather. I grew up in Southern California and didn't know much about it.

So a little while ago I put a wool hat on my head and my feet aren't cold any more.

What else? It's such a valuable question. It is especially useful when you've been doing something a certain way for a long time.

I'm always surprised when someone comes up with a new way to do something familiar, because it makes me think, "Now why didn't I think of that?" Once you see the new way, it seems kind of obvious. But it took somebody asking "What else?" to come up with it.

"Unaware of Mind's effect in patterning and enslaving their lives," wrote William Bartley III, "people live in a state of waking sleep, in a state of enchantment, of mesmerism, most of the time. Every day, in every way, they become more and more the way they have always been."

A couple of days ago I saw measuring spoons, but rather than having a separate spoon for teaspoons and tablespoons and halves and fourths, it was a single spoon with one end of the cupped part capable of sliding back and fourth, making the cup bigger or smaller, and there were lines on it for teaspoon and half teaspoon, etc.

Why didn't I think of that? Because I didn't ask, "*What else* could measure teaspoons besides the measuring spoon I'm so familiar with?"

"What else?" is especially practical when what you usually do doesn't work very well. When a particular person makes certain kinds of remarks, you *could* get angry and defend yourself, but *what else* could you do?

You can do a certain task grudgingly, but how *else* could you do it? What other ways could you go about it? In what other ways could you *think* about it?

When you interact with your teenager and you both end up angry, ask yourself, "What *else* could I do?" What other approaches or responses can you think up besides what you normally do?

Here's a good rule: If what you're doing isn't working, do something else.

Of course, you don't want to go with something *just* because it's different, because the new idea could be *worse*.

Creativity is the process of thinking up new ideas and then rejecting most of them. But those are two processes, and the parts of your brains involved in each are different, so they shouldn't be done at the same time.

In other words, when you're thinking up alternatives, don't judge the ideas for their merits at the same time. Let your mind go. Let it come up with crazy ideas, off-the-wall angles, impossible notions. This stretches your mind beyond the limits which has previously confined your thinking. Out of that loosened-up state of mind, a truly original idea and sometimes a perfect solution can suddenly become obvious. You just couldn't see it before because you were unknowingly confining your thinking about that subject within certain parameters.

Think up ideas, and keep thinking them up until you get a good one. And if it's important enough, and you have the time, keep thinking up ideas and see if you can come up with an even *better* one.

After you've thought up all the ideas you want, then *and only then*, judge the ideas for their merit. Do not do the creative part and the judging part simultaneously because it will interfere with your ability to think up novel out-of-the-box ideas.

The best way to characterize "thinking" is as a dialog. Consider thinking as a dialog with yourself. I know that if it is with yourself it's supposed to be called a monologue, but thinking isn't done very well as a monologue because there is nothing to provoke the thoughts further. A monologue is an expression of an already-decided thought. Dialog can create something new.

Have a thought and then criticize it and you have a dialog. Come up with an idea and then ask, "What else?" and you have dialog, and that's where good thinking happens.

"Well, my in-laws are coming over," says Pete to himself, "and they always drive me nuts. Every time I open my mouth, they make me sorry I said anything. Maybe I'll just not say anything."

If Pete stops there, his monologue has created one idea. But this time he has a dialog with himself, and thereby becomes more creative. "Yes, I could try that," he says to himself, "but what else might work?"

"What else might work for what?" he asks himself. "I guess I need a goal if I want to think up an idea to solve it. I need to know what I'm trying to accomplish."

"I want to feel happy even when they are here," he decides.

"Do I feel happy when I say nothing?"

"No. I've tried that before. It's not much fun. It's a little better than being annoyed, but I'm definitely not happy."

"So what *else* could I do?"

"Since I want to be happy," he answers himself, "I should do what makes me happy. I really enjoy playing my new video game. Maybe I can enlist one of them to play with me."

"Good idea. But I'm not going to stop there. What *else* could I do?"

"I like talking about politics. I could make that my theme for the night. I could turn every conversation to the subject of politics."

"That's not bad. What else could I do?"

And so on. The more Pete asks, the more ideas he will get. Some of his ideas will be goofy or won't work very well, but thinking is like good photography: You take lots of pictures and then get rid of almost all of them. You'll have maybe two or three good ones, but they were worth it.

Creativity is like that. You generate lots of ideas and throw out most of them. But in generating so many, you have more to choose from, so your chances of getting a better one improve as the number of ideas increases. And the way to get many ideas is to keep asking, "What else?"

What Memory Makes Me Feel Good?

You have good memories, and they can make you feel good, but only if you recall them. You could have a fantastic memory that you never reminisce about and you can forget it ever happened! In fact, it is almost for sure you have many wonderful moments you've already forgotten. Some of them might be recent. The event happened, it was great, but life moves on and you haven't thought of it since. That memory is on its way to being forgotten.

But not if you ask yourself this question occasionally: What memory makes me feel good?

Every time you remember something, you strengthen the memory. When you don't recall a memory, it tends to fade away unless it was emotionally significant, and even then a strong memory is not guaranteed.

Depressed people have just as many positive events as non-depressed people, according to the research, but depressed people reminisce more about their negative events. They strengthen those memories so they seem more real, they seem more numerous, they appear more vivid, and they are easier to recall again because they've been recalled before.

You can use this same method in reverse and you will feel better more often. Your life will feel richer and more wonderful because your memory will be full of easily-recalled great times. You will have more confidence in yourself because you'll remember more of your triumphs and successes. You'll feel more in love because you'll remember more of those special moments you've had with your mate.

Ask yourself the question and ponder it. You'll be happier.

Ask Questions to Find Out More About the Situation

Al Siebert has spent 40 years interviewing survivors of all kinds to find out what makes them different from people who don't survive difficult situations. One of his discoveries is survivors tend to be curious. They ask questions about their situation.

Often people who didn't survive tried to impose their own "shoulds" on the situation: People should act this way; nobody should be allowed to be so brutal; nobody should have to eat food with weevils in it. Rather than opening their minds to the way things were really working, they pointlessly occupied their minds with fruitless indignation at what should not be.

Survivors on the other hand, says Siebert, asked themselves questions like, "What is going on here?" "How do the guards see this?" "What must I do to give myself a chance to survive?" They were curious, open, and inquisitive.

This kind of questioning is good for a great many applications besides surviving in a POW camp: at work, in your marriage, with your kids. Find out how things work, what's going on, who responds to what, what people are feeling and why, etc., etc. There is so much to know and so little time. So open your eyes and ears and start asking some good questions.

What if it Really Happened?

Edna Foa conducted research on social anxiety to find out what helped the most to reduce anxiety. The answer was changing the way a person thought about *consequences*. That was the key to whether someone succeeded or failed to manage their anxiety.

Specifically, anxious people expect the consequences of a negative event to be worse than they would actually be. And of course this makes them more anxious than they need to be.

When you worry about something, you're asking yourself, "What if?" You wonder, What if X happened? And you think the consequences would be terrible. That's what scares you. What if it happened?

What I've discovered I do (and apparently I'm not alone) is stop right there. I don't think beyond it. I worry, "What if that happened?" and it scares me so much I don't want to think any more about it. But when I make myself follow through on the question, my anxiety is usually cured in short order. Let me give you an example.

When my wife and I first got married, whenever we had an argument, it made me very upset. I was always afraid the argument would bring our relationship to an end. My question was, "What if she leaves me?" It sounds stupid now, but I never once thought beyond that. It was too awful to contemplate. This is the woman with whom I share all my dreams. This is my best friend. This is the one I love with all my heart. It was too terrifying to think any further than her leaving me.

This worry put me in a panic, and usually my desperation to prevent an impending disaster would only make our fights worse. I wouldn't let us take a break. She wanted to leave and go for a walk. I wouldn't let her go until we had resolved our argument. Of course, it is almost impossible to resolve an argument between two people when both are upset, so my actions prolonged our arguments and made them more destructtive.

One day I asked her how she managed to stay so calm when we argued. I always seemed to get intense, but even when she was mad, she never got anxious or desperate.

"Do any thoughts go through your mind when we're arguing?" I asked, "Do you say anything to yourself? Do you picture something?"

Turns out, she did something very specific. She did it every time and it kept her calm. She never thought of it as a "technique." Like me, she also had the thought, "What if this is the end of us?" But she didn't stop there. Rather than recoiling from the thought, she faced it. She deliberately imagined the worst that could happen. She tried to see a little movie in her mind of what would happen if we divorced. She imagined going through the sadness, moving to a different place, and going on with her life.

And as she imagined time passing, she could see that she would survive, and even if this tragic thing happened, there would actually be some happiness down the road.

This seemed like a pretty straightforward technique, so I gave it a try and it really calmed me down. Our fights became less intense because I wasn't trying so hard to stop the fight (try to end an argument quickly and it will often make the fight last longer).

Imagining the worst does two things: First of all, imagining a divorce and us moving away from each other always makes me sad. No matter how angry I am when I start thinking about it, I always feel sad because I realize how much I would miss her. That is a good realization to have during a fight. It's a perspective that sometimes goes out the window when I'm angry, and it's worth remembering.

The second benefit is realizing that even if this worst-case-scenario happened, I could still go on and be happy. That helps me keep the situation in perspective and helps me calm down. And my lower anxiety helps me listen. It helps me speak more calmly and kindly and sanely.

I tried it the very next time we had an argument. It worked beautifully. It may have been the first time we ever argued when I stayed relatively calm. I didn't panic at all. I didn't get desperate. I tried it again the next argument. And the next. And that's about all it took. That was more than 25 years ago, and I now never even consider the possibility that an argument spells doom. It totally cured me of that particular anxiety.

All I did was think beyond the original fear. Try it with one of your fears right now. You're afraid of what? What makes you afraid when you think about it?

What if it happened? Really, think about it. What if that terrible thing really happened? What would come next? And then what? And then what?

Jim says, "I get nervous at work because I'm afraid my boss is going to get mad at me."

I say, "Okay, what if he does?"

Jim: "It would be upsetting."

Me: "Yeah, so? Then what would happen?"

Jim: "He might write me up. That means it would be a warning, and one more and I'll be fired!"

Me: "Okay, let's say that happens. He writes you up, you don't improve, and then he fires you. Then what would you do?"

Jim: "I'd have to find another job."

Me: "Okay. Could you do that?"

Jim: "Yeah, I think so, but it might not pay as much as I'm making now."

Me: "So, what would you do then?"

Jim: "I'd have to buy fewer things."

When you follow the line of questioning, it always seems to peter out into nothing. You realize you could handle it. You'd live. It wouldn't be catastrophic. It may be difficult. It may be inconvenient. It may be a challenge. But it's nothing to get distraught over.

According to the research, the two biggest mistakes anxious people tend to make is that they think the bad thing is more *likely* than it really is, and they think if the bad thing happens, the *consequences* would be more horrible than they really would be.

This is the antidote: Ask the question, "What would happen then?" and keep following the realistic consequences out to their probable natural conclusion, and your fear usually fades or disappears.

I need to warn you about something. Please remember this: It won't work to tell yourself, "It'll be okay." I've tried it and it doesn't have any impact on my anxiety. You *must* go through the visualization. You must see it happening and see how you'd handle it. Be honest in your imaginings. Try to make it true-to-life. Don't try to imagine it more positively than you really think would happen. That's not the point. What do you think would *really* happen? Imagine it. And what do you think you'd really do about it? This will have a definite — and maybe even a dramatic — effect on your feelings.

Like a magic bullet, it goes to the heart of your worry and dissolves it.

In his book, *How to Stop Worrying and Start Living*, Dale Carnegie tells the story of a man who cured himself of a very serious case of anxiety using a method very similar to this. His name was Earl Haney and he had ulcers. Bad ulcers.

One night Haney had a hemorrhage and was rushed to the hospital where he stayed. He had holes in his stomach lining and had to have his stomach pumped every day. His diet was alkaline powder and a tablespoon of half-and-half per hour. He was in bad shape.

This continued for several months. His weight dropped from 175 pounds to 90 pounds. Three doctors agreed he was terminal. Death was inevitable. He was basically waiting around to die.

Then a thought dawned on Haney. He realized he had always wanted to travel the world before he died and he figured if he was going to do it, he'd better go now.

Of course, his doctors were strongly against the idea. Haney would have to pump his own stomach twice a day. Crazy!

Haney went ahead with his plans anyway. He even bought a casket and took it with him so if he died on the way, he could be buried in the family plot back home.

He boarded a ship from Los Angeles to visit China and India. During the voyage, he gradually gave up on all the pampering and stomach pumping. He let it go. If he was going to die, so be it, he thought. His worry and tension evaporated. He stopped worrying.

Even during a typhoon, which should have scared him to death, he actually enjoyed it because he had already looked at the "what if." It didn't bother him.

He'd looked at the consequences already: He would die and his body would be sent back to Nebraska. His alternative was wasting away in a hospital, and he'd much rather die in a typhoon on his way to China.

He started really enjoying himself now that he was free of constant worries, and he gained 90 pounds on his trip. His health returned. When he got home, he went back to work and never felt better in his life.

He was cured. He stopped cowering in fear at what might happen. He had learned to take an honest, unflinching look at the likely consequences of possible negative events. The constant worry evaporated into the thin air it was made of.

You can have the same sort of recovery from your worry. Think about something you have worried about recently. Now ask yourself, "What if it happened?" Really. What if it happened? What would you do about it? How would you respond? And *then* what would happen? And then what? And how would you respond to that? Follow it through as realistically as you can and see if that doesn't have a dramatic effect on that particular worry.

When your own distress is making things worse, go ahead and confront the worst that could possibly happen. Don't just do it briefly. This isn't positive thinking. Don't merely tell yourself, "Oh, there is nothing to be afraid of, everything will be all right." That won't work! Imagine the worst case scenario clearly in your mind. Imagine what would happen. Imagine time passing. And be realistic. Don't try to be optimistic with your imaginings. Try to imagine what you really think would happen.

What you will discover is that this is not the calamity you feared. And your increased calm will help make a calamity less likely.

What Am I Good At?

The best way to direct your mind is with a good question. Ask yourself a question and ask it again and again. Make up your own question or use one of the questions here. And one very good question to ponder is, "What am I good at?"

Recalling your own abilities helps nurture and strengthen those abilities (making you more capable of getting things done) and it also makes you feel better about yourself to remember what you're good at. Try it right now and you'll feel noticeably better almost immediately. Technically, you may "already know" your strengths. But if you took five minutes and thought up four of your greatest strengths right now, you would feel noticeably better. You'd feel stronger and more capable, and those are useful feelings to experience.

You have strengths you take for granted. But if you suddenly didn't have one of your strengths, you would sorely miss it. Recognize that simple fact, and appreciate what you have by asking this question: *What abilities do I have?* Ponder it. Write down your answers. Make a list, and as you think of more, keep adding to the list.

If you think about this in your head, your thoughts will tend to drift toward your weaknesses and the mistakes you've made because of your brain's automatic negative bias (read more about that in the book, *Antivirus for the Mind*). To help you focus on the question, use paper and pen and set a target: Either set a timer or aim for coming up with a definite number of answers.

In other words, set a timer for say, twenty minutes, and keep coming up with answers until the timer goes off. Or write at the top of a piece of paper: Ten things I'm good at. Then don't stop until you write down ten. Forcing yourself in this way squeezes out good answers you might not otherwise come up with.

Do this exercise and you will feel better. That kind of positive emotion is good for your health. Not only will it make you feel better, but it helps you realize what you are especially good at, and it will encourage you to do more of it.

Brian Tracy, Alan Laiken and many other experts on accomplishment have pointed out that if you are not very good at accounting but you're great at selling, you'll make more money and have more fun in the long run if you spend the money to pay an accountant so you can spend more time selling. Find out what your abilities are and you'll find it easier to focus on what you're good at.

It may not be a good idea to brag to others about your special qualities, but it is very good for *you* to acknowledge your abilities to yourself. False internal humility in the privacy of your own mind is really a form of lying to yourself, and self-deception of this kind is not good for you.

Ask yourself the questions, "What abilities do I have?" and "What am I good at?" Becoming more aware of your abilities makes you saner, healthier, and stronger. You'll feel better and get more done.

You can find out your "signature strengths" by taking the VIA Signature Strengths Questionnaire at AuthenticHappiness.org. A signature strength is a character trait or virtue that you habitually display and enjoy expressing.

What is One Healthy Thing I Could Do Today to Feel Better?

You have control over your mood to a degree you might find surprising. Anything from taking a nap to having a snack to writing down what you're grateful for can make you feel better in a very short time.

Some people are hesitant to improve their mood. People have told me before, "that's just the way I feel right now," and imply that if they were to try to change their mood it would be dishonest. Hogwash. They clearly haven't thought that one through. Your mood changes like the weather. You are not your moods any more than you are the water that moves through your body.

It would be similar to saying, "My body just stinks. That's the way I smell right now," and that is your reason for not showering. As if showering would be dishonest. It's just stupid. If you don't want to put out any effort to feel better just because it feels better, then think about doing it for your better health. Or do it because it will improve the moods of those around you. Or because it makes you more effective in dealing with people. Or because it will improve your ability to solve problems. There are many good reasons to improve your mood and no good reason to continue in a bad mood when you can easily change it.

One man told me it bothered him that when he was at work and he was in a bad mood, his co-workers didn't like it. "I feel like I'm obligated to pretend to feel good when I don't."

"What makes you think you're obligated," I asked.

"I don't know," he sighed, "they try to cheer me up, or they give me a bad time about being grumpy, or they get short-tempered with me like they're mad at me for not feeling good."

"That's interesting," I said. "I remember reading a study on charisma. They had three people in a room just sit there. One of them was naturally charismatic, and the other two were not. They were told to just sit there and not say anything for a little while. At the end of that short time, without saying a word, the moods of the two less-charismatic people had moved toward the mood of the charismatic person."

He looked puzzled.

95

"In other words," I explained, "They tested the moods of all three before and after sitting in the room together. Let's say the charismatic person was feeling irritable beforehand. Maybe one of the other people was feeling cheerful. After sitting in the room, the cheerful (but uncharismatic) person was more irritable.

"All I'm saying is that moods are contagious, and that is especially so when someone is charismatic, like yourself. So probably when you're in a bad mood, it starts ruining the moods of the people around you and they are resisting that."

"What, so I'm responsible for their moods now?" He didn't seem too happy about this.

"There is some good and bad to just about anything. When you're charismatic, it's great because you make friends easily, people are attracted to you, you're more persuasive, you have more influence on others, and so on. On the other hand, people pay more attention to your moods and that may seem like a burden, but it is nothing more than being in a position of leadership. Charisma is a power. And like the uncle in *Spiderman* said, 'With great power comes great responsibility.'"

He laughed but he got the point too. And I hope you do too.

Whatever the cause of your mood, it is almost always true that you can do something about it. If you feel stressed, you can meditate or do some aerobic exercise. If you feel like you have no energy you could have a cup of coffee or go for a walk or take a nap. If you feel angry, you could use the antivirus for the mind or write in a diary or talk to a friend. If you feel lonely, you could reach out and communicate with someone or read a good book on relationships.

Ask yourself how you can improve your mood at the moment, and keep asking until you come up with some good answers, and then pick one and do it.

When you want to improve your mood, simply ask the question: What's one healthy thing I could do today to feel better?

What Needs to be Done Next?

We're looking at different questions you can use to direct your mind. This one will help you stay productive, especially in a distracting environment or if you feel upset. It is good all by itself, but I often add a little statement to the front of it when I use it myself. I say: "That's not worth the attention; what am I doing next?" In your life, you know some people irritate you, some kinds of circumstances annoy you, and there are things that make you angry. When something bothers you, you have a choice: You can do something about it or leave it behind you. This question is for the things you aren't willing to do anything about (or *can't* do anything about).

There's no sense in even thinking about something if you can't do anything about it or aren't *willing* to do anything about it. That's easy enough to say, but the problem is, of course, that our minds tend to stick on things like that, don't they? If something seems unjust or wrong, it's hard to get it out of your mind. Negative feelings compel your attention. The *feelings* arrest your attention, and generate *thoughts* that arrest your attention too, even when you've already decided not to do anything about it.

It takes a firm act of will to unstick your mind and go on about your life, but it's an extremely useful ability to have. Get in the habit of not ever dwelling on something you can't do anything about. Train yourself to redirect your mind to something productive. How? By asking yourself the question: "What needs to be done next?" Or, "That's not worth the attention; what am I doing next?"

Attention is your main resource. It's really all you have that's worth anything. So when your attention is consumed by useless thoughts or feelings or actions, you're throwing pieces of your life down the drain, and there are so many good things you could be doing with your attention.

There are more things, subjects, people of a positive nature than you could ever put your attention on. Why waste it on something negative unless you want to, or unless it serves you?

Say there are ten billion potential objects of attention available in the world at any one time. But you are limited. You have only so much time. You can pay attention to only so many things at once. For the sake of argument, let's say you have only a hundred available units of attention at any given moment. There are ten billion objects available, but you can only partake of a hundred. Why take fifty or even ten of your hundred units and waste them on something unproductively negative?

What would you think about someone who had a hundred dollars and spent ten dollars buying something she didn't want, even though there were at least a million dollars worth of things she really *did* want? You would think she was foolishly wasting her money, right?

You can put a stop to the waste of your attention. Say to yourself: "That's not worth the attention; what am I doing next?" Use the question to plug the leaks in your bucket.

Your mind is attracted to certain things, compelled by certain feelings, some of which are negative and harmful. And your mind doesn't change direction easily. The machinery of your mind, if we can call it that, is stubborn. But you don't have to put up with it. Start saying to yourself today, "That's not worth the attention; what am I doing next?" and don't stop until a new habit is formed.

Start with little things, and when the big things come along, you'll have the resources to deal with them. As William James wrote:

So with the man who has daily inured himself
to habits of concentrated attention, energetic
volition, and self-denial in unnecessary things.
He will stand like a tower when everything

rocks around him, and when his softer fellow mortals are winnowed like chaff in the blast.

Use this question and use it often and you will have power and self-control far beyond your peers. But here let me issue the following clarification: This statement-plus-question (that's not worth the attention; what am I doing next?) shouldn't be applied to certain things.

If you have a drinking problem, for example, and it's destroying your health and your relationships and your financial future, you can do something about it, so this statement-plus-question is not applicable.

If you are experiencing grief because a loved one just died, your grief is worth your attention. It is healthy to grieve and unhealthy to suppress it. And there is something you can do about it. You can't bring your loved-one back, but you can talk to someone about it. You can write about your pain in a journal. People who do these things after a big loss are healthier in the long run than people who don't.

Dale Larson, PhD, and his research team at Santa Clara University surveyed close to 300 people about events in their lives they considered shameful or painful, and also about how much of these things they kept to themselves or shared with other people.

The researchers then looked at the volunteers' records of mental and physical health problems. Of course, those who experienced severely stressful things like losing a parent as a child or rape, experienced more health problems, but the problems were significantly reduced in those who had talked about it than those who kept it a secret.

And in general, those who tended to keep painful or shameful experiences to themselves suffered more headaches, fatigue, and indigestion than those who had a tendency to confide things with a trusted friend.

James Pennebaker, PhD, who has done a tremendous amount of research on this subject, says, "not discussing or confiding [a traumatic] event with another may be more damaging than having experienced the event *per se*."

Apparently, holding things in is a kind of psychological "work" and it's a strain on your system to do it.

I should point out that it doesn't work to share your pain with just anybody and everybody. If you're going to talk, talk to a trusted friend, someone you know won't share it with anyone else and who will not criticize you or make fun of you, but will listen. Or, as Pennebaker has found, it even works to write it in a journal.

This statement-plus-question (that's not worth the attention; what am I doing next?) is to use for the annoyances and frustrations of daily life, including the people in your life who like to mess with your head or who seem to deliberately try to make you unhappy.

Did you think you were the only one? Think again, my friend. We all have people in our lives who seem to act like friends, but bring us down in one way or another.

The author of *Little Women*, Louisa May Alcott was once given this friendly advice: Find work as a seamstress or servant.

You've probably heard of Vince Lombardi. He's one of the most famous football coaches in the history of the sport. An expert once said of him, "He possess-es minimal football knowledge. Lacks motivation."

In 1933 Fred Astaire had his first screen test. The testing director summarized Astaire like this: "Can't act. Slightly bald. Can dance a little."

The better you are, the more you accomplish, the more people will try to bring you down. That's just the way it is and there's nothing you can do to change that reality. You can, however, respond to it any way you choose.

I want you to remember something: Life is only so long, and then it's over. Don't waste precious mom-ents. Don't throw away your attention.

I know a woman who brings up bad news every time you talk to her. She reads the newspaper, and whenever there's something particularly tragic or ter-rible, it obviously sticks in her mind, as it would most normal people. I don't read newspapers for that very reason: I don't want things like that stuck in my mind. There's nothing I can do about a car accident that hap-pened yesterday.

This woman brings up bad news, and doesn't just mention it, but goes into graphic detail, and she's skilled enough to give you a sharp, full-color image of the tragedy in all its vivid sadness.

When she talks to me, she gives me things that compete with other thoughts, images, ideas. There's a limit to how many thoughts I can hold. The same goes for you. Our capacity for attention is limited. Even if we're much better than average, we can only hold so many thoughts at once. So in this sense, thoughts are in competition for our attention.

Graphic, compelling, tragic thoughts compete very effectively because strong emotions demand attention. I used to listen to this woman, but then I realized something important: When she shared her news, it served her goals, but not mine.

Now as soon as the headline comes out of her mouth, I change the subject. I don't let her fill me in on the graphic details. Luckily, I don't have to talk to her much. But it's an example of how some things that compel your attention very strongly don't necessarily help you. Giving them your attention may serve someone else, but it only poured your precious moments down the drain.

The same holds true when the thought has not been put there by someone else. The human mind is incredibly full. Your mind can wander far and wide, and sometimes it stumbles upon a worry or fear, and even though it may be an emotionally gripping thought, that doesn't mean it has to be thought through, figured out, or solved.

When something is emotionally commanding, it often feels as if the thought is clamoring very loudly for your attention, like a baby crying or loud moans of pain from someone nearby, but the feeling may have nothing to do with the worthiness of the thought itself.

After I decided to write books for a living, I was often haunted by the worry: "What if I never make it? What if nobody wants to buy my books? What if I try and try and I go broke and wind up a penniless street person and die of cold in some gutter as an old man?"

Somewhere along the way, probably in a fit of despair, I created that vivid mental image and it was compelling for emotional reasons. But it was a stupid thing to think. Yes, the book business is not as "secure" as some other fields, but I had made up my mind to do it, so this kind of worrying was not doing me any good.

This statement-plus-question (that's not worth the attention; what am I doing next?) put my mind on a new track. When I get that image now of being a penniless street person lying in a gutter, this statement-plus-question is fast on its heels, and it happens so quickly now, the image has begun to motivate me and increase my determination.

How?

Because of the question: "What am I doing next?" Because of the haunting image, what I want to do next is work on becoming successful in the book business! I want to make sure I don't goof off. It motivates me to burn the midnight oil. As soon as my thoughts turn to what I need to do, I am off and running and forget about the worries. I'm too busy making it happen to worry about whether it's going to happen or not.

This is totally different from what used to happen. The image used to bring me down. The image was compelling because it was me in the image, and I was afraid of it. It was like a leach, sucking my lifeblood (my attention) and contributing nothing to me. It was a parasitic thought.

And what is the best thing to do with a parasite? Kill it. If you had a tick or a leach or an intestinal worm, you wouldn't hesitate to cut its life short. Mercy or compassion for a parasite would be stupid. It's leaching off of you. It is taking your life, your energy, your attention, and only taking. Giving you nothing.

When you have a thought in that category, show no mercy, show no coddling, and do not play around: Cut it off without delay.

And the way to cut off a thought, the way to kill it, is to replace it with a better one. The mind won't remain empty for long. You can't just stop thinking something. You have to have something better to think instead. It is counterproductive to try not to think something.

Two researchers from the University of Virginia — Daniel Wegner and Daniel Gold — told 110 female and male subjects to think about a past lover who they still desired. Then they were given eight minutes. Half of them were told to continue to think about the lover. The other half were told to suppress thoughts of their previous lover — to not think of them at all for the eight minutes.

Then the researchers hooked everyone up to a device that measures emotional reactions. It measured how much sweat they produced on the surface of their fingers, and the subjects were told to think about their former sweethearts again. Those who had spent eight minutes trying to get their old flames out of their minds had a much stronger emotional reaction.

One of the researchers, Daniel M. Wegner, PhD, is somewhat famous in psychology circles for his many experiments showing what happens when you suppress a thought: It makes the thought more intense and obsessional. Some of his earlier experiments went like this: He put people in a room with a tape recorder and told them to speak aloud whatever was on their minds, except for one thing — under no circumstances were they to think about a white bear.

The tape recorded their ongoing thoughts, which included something about a white bear, on average, about once a minute. There are billions of things to think about, but their minds kept coming back to the one thought they were trying not to think. They tried as many mental tricks as they could come up with, but the thought of a white bear kept coming back to them.

When you say to yourself, "That's not worth the attention; what am I doing next?" you are putting your mind on something else instead of trying not to think something. And it works.

Do this often enough, and even a thought that used to haunt you often could begin to remind you to think the new thought. After awhile, your mind will start to streamline the process and skip right over the old thought, and at that point you've effectively choked off its lifeblood (the attention it was draining from your life). It only lives by your attention, and when it no longer gets any attention, it is dead.

And when it is dead, you have just gained more life.

The question, "What needs to be done next?" is also good on its own. It gets your mind thinking productively, no matter what's happening. It can help you pull yourself out of a bad mood. It can help you get back on track. Try it today.

What Good Have I Been Ignoring?

We are nearing the end of my list of recommended questions to ask. Remember, the principle is to direct your mind by using a good question. This question is one of my favorites. What good have I been ignoring? The answers go on and on, improving my mood the whole time. You will keep thinking of more and more good things you've been ignoring. The question almost demands it.

The emotional fallout from this question is abundant good feelings of happiness, gratitude, and pleasant surprise. When you ask a question like this, you'll find answers everywhere. The question makes you look. You'll realize someone has done something nice for you and you hadn't really noticed. You will remember a great time you had a couple weeks ago and realize you hadn't thought of it since then.

The question sets your mind to be on the lookout for good you've overlooked. You'll notice good news items you might not normally notice, like how this lake got cleaned up or that disease now has a cure. The question helps overcome a natural tendency of the mind to get used to good things and only notice bad things.

What has been improving? What's been getting better?

Ask this question, think of some answers, and ask it again.

This is especially a good question to ask if you've had your attention on what has been getting worse, or if you've had a feeling things are going badly, or you're worried they will go badly.

This question won't solve all your problems, of course, but it can reduce the amount of distress you're feeling by widening the tunnel vision stress causes. You are not trying to fool yourself or pretend everything is rosy. You're looking to acknowledge the reality of what has been getting better.

When those are acknowledged, you are less distressed and more able to make things even better. And it is good for your mood. A good mood is healthy and productive. What good have *you* been ignoring?

How Can I Look at This as a Good Thing?

On an old radio show, back in the days before television, *The Amos and Andy Show* was extremely popular. It was a comedy show, but sometimes they said something profound. In one show, Amos asked the Kingfish why he had such good judgment. The Kingfish replied, "Well, good judgment comes from experience."

"Then," asked Amos, "where does experience come from?"

"From bad judgment," answered the Kingfish.

There's always something to learn from misfortune. And that's what this chapter is about: Dealing with adversity and setbacks. Dealing with events you didn't want to happen.

The Kingfish pointed out one way you can always look at a setback as a good thing: You can learn something from it. At the very least, you can learn how to avoid having the same setback twice. But if you use your imagination, you can do better than that. Before you even see how something turns out, you can find ways of looking at an event that would make you feel good about it, even when it is obviously bad.

I'll give you some examples in a minute, but I want you to see that if a "bad" thing has already happened, there's no point in thinking of it as bad. Thinking it's bad doesn't help you to correct the problem, if it can be corrected. And if it can't be corrected, it still doesn't help you to think of it as a bad thing. People can learn and remember just fine when they feel good. You do not have to feel bad to learn from your mistakes. In fact, people tend to learn better in a positive frame of mind than a negative one.

So there is no good reason to ever hold onto the judgment of a situation or event in your life as bad, awful, terrible, tragic, unfortunate, or lousy. It doesn't do you any good to consider an event that has already happened to be bad.

You can find a way to look at anything that happens to you as good, and people who are habitually successful and happy do exactly that. You notice I said "anything that happens to *you*." If someone you love dies, do not try to see it as good. You probably would not anyway, but this is a disclaimer to let you know I'm not a nutcase. When something terrible happens to someone you care about, this question is probably not appropriate. The question is for events that happen to you personally.

Sometimes you'll hear someone say, "I'm glad that terrible accident happened to me; it made me aware that my priorities were wrong." And people who find meaning and value in even "bad" things in their lives are happier and more successful than those who just think it was a terrible misfortune.

And it's not a matter of *chance* which way they look at it. It's up to each person to decide how they will look at their circumstances. We have the choice, and we will live with the feelings that spring out of the choices we make.

If we take the easy way and choose to look at a "bad" thing as bad, we'll get the results of the easy way: Bad feelings. But if we use our heads with a little more vigor, if we make the effort to actively look for what's good about it, if we choose to find a way to look at it as a positive thing, we will get the results of that choice too: It'll be easier to wake up in the morning, we will be nicer to the people we love, we will take advantage of what we have in our lives, and we will feel better in general.

You can ask yourself, *How can I look at this as a good thing?* Or you can simply assert to yourself, *This is good!* and then ask yourself *why* it's good. Declare it's good, and then allow your mind to find how you're right. Either way works well.

Try it right now. Think of something in your life that you consider "bad." It could be a condition you've lived with for some time, or something that happened recently you don't like and wished hadn't happened.

I'll go along with you. I was a little curt with my sister-in-law, and now she's not talking to me. Obviously that's bad. Any idiot can see it's bad. Only a starry-eyed goober would say that's *good*. But I'm going to try to see what's good about it. And come along with me, bringing the thing you think is bad with you. How can you look at it as a good thing?

How can I see it as *good* that I have this situation with my sister-in-law? Well, I can see right off the bat, I get to use it as an example in this chapter. Not only that, but it may be an opportunity to apply some of the *other* principles in my toolbox and might give me some good examples for those also.

How else? Hmm. Well, I really haven't gotten to know my sister-in-law very well as of yet, mainly because we live in different cities. And I know that sometimes in working out a conflict, people get to know each other a lot better, and there's no reason to think this won't happen with us. I can see it as good because it is an opportunity for us to get to know each other better, and at a deeper, less superficial level.

How else can I look at it as a good thing?

What about you? Have you found ways to look at yours is a good thing? Be creative. Look at it from outside your own perspective. If a professor of psychology knew about your situation, assume she could see it as good. How would she explain her position to you?

If everything is easy, I have no opportunity to apply what I've learned. In applying what I've learned, I learn it better. In handling a difficult situation, I can take knowledge and turn it into skill. From this perspective, anything difficult is good. Friedrich Nietzsche said, "That which does not kill me makes me strong." Although that statement isn't strictly true, the attitude is a good perspective to adopt when difficulties come your way.

I tell you truthfully, if you make these principles a part of your thinking, you'll be insuppressible, unstoppable, and you will feel pretty good almost all the time. No kidding. The way you think makes a big difference. And each principle is like another plug in the bottom of your bucket. Less and less of your happiness leaks out as more and more of these principles become a part of your thinking.

I know that some of them are already a part of your thinking, although you probably don't have them worded exactly this way. I haven't put in principles like "I can change my own life for the better" because you already think that way or you wouldn't be reading this book. You already think in a healthier way than many people who wouldn't bother looking reading this book because they think "I'm just the way I am and I can never change."

You also already know that even if you're doing better than most, you can always get better. And each new principle, repeated many times, is a solid step in that direction. This one (How can I look at this as a good thing?) is extremely useful.

This is a principle of thought. And thinking is at its most creative when it is a dialog — specifically, asking and answering questions. That's how to do your most productive creative thinking: Ask yourself a question and then try to answer it.

For example, Sylvia has just been fired. She's on her way home from her ex-job. But she asks herself, almost with bitter sarcasm at first, "How can I look at this as a good thing?"

Sometimes when your body is filled with a negative emotion, a question like this won't have a good effect right away. Don't give up. Ask it again. And again.

"This isn't a good thing," thinks Sylvia, "not a good thing at all. 'But how can I *look* at this as a good thing?'" She just needs to keep asking. She needs to awaken the part of her brain that answers questions.

And it is awake! "Maybe I'll get a better job," she says to herself without much conviction.

Ask it again! *Keep* asking the question. Sylvia does, and her mind turns more and more to the question, and it stops mulling her misfortune and stops moaning about how wronged she has been, and turns slowly toward the question. Then her mind kicks in and starts bringing up answers, slowly at first, and then faster and faster.

"There were a lot of things I didn't like about that job. Now I have an opportunity to start over. It's a good thing I got fired. I should have moved on from there long ago, but I guess I was just being lazy. This might be the best thing that could have happened to me. Maybe I should sit down and carefully decide what kind of job I want to get, and what kind of company I'd like to work for..."

And so on. Once the mind gets going, it can really come up with some good stuff.

Ask yourself: *How can I look at this as a good thing?* And keep asking.

What Could I Do to Make Some Progress on my Goal?

O ne of the most important things in your life is having a purpose. And one of the best ways to feel better and have a more meaningful, fulfilling existence is to make progress toward your goal. Chores and distractions, however, can easily absorb so much of your time that you never get around to doing something toward your most important goal. That's frustrating, and it brings you down, which makes you less motivated to work on your goal. It makes you less motivated to do the one thing almost guaranteed to bring you up.

This question — what could you do to make some progress on your goal — focuses your attention on something that will make a difference to you right now *and* in the long run. It makes you feel better immediately to make progress on a goal. And the ultimate achievement of your goal will make a difference to you in the long run.

And all you need to do is make some progress. It's not either you work for ten hours on your goal or you can't do anything about it. You can almost always do *something* that will make *some* progress toward your goal, and a little is much better than nothing. The question is what could you do, not what would be the most ideal if everything were perfect. If you think of something and it would take three hours and you only have fifteen minutes, *keep thinking*. What *could* you do?

Try it right now. What could you do to make even a little progress on your most important goal?

Could I Just Do Part
Of It For Now?

The time-management expert, Alan Lakein, calls this the "Swiss Cheese" method. You poke a hole in your project. After you poke enough holes in a project, there isn't much left. A large project becomes easier and easier to tackle the more holes you poke in it. Also, when you don't have the time or motivation to tackle your project, you can do some small thing that moves it forward, even a little, and that will do two things: It'll improve your mood, and it will make the project a little less intimidating.

This question keeps you moving. It keeps you making progress.

One of Lakein's techniques is to set a timer for five minutes, and work on your project until the time is up. Because it is so brief, you are not at all intimidated.

Five minutes. You can stand just about anything for five measly minutes.

Often you'll find that once your five minutes are up, you don't really want to stop. But by giving yourself such a small goal to begin with, you are able to get *something* done. Without that technique, you would have gotten nothing done on that project.

And working on your project for even five minutes gets you thinking about it, which is usually a good thing.

We tend to think about projects as a whole. This question gets us thinking about doing smaller parts of the whole. Do you have a large project you've been putting off because it's such a large project and you don't want to get started? Ponder this question. Can you do something on it for five minutes? Can you do a small part of it now?

What Would Be a More Reasonable Explanation?

Whenever a setback or failure occurs, you will explain it. You can't help it. Your explanation will come quickly and automatically. And your explanation will seem entirely self-evident. (Learn more about that in the book, *Antivirus For Your Mind.*) Some of your explanations are good, some will make you feel bad unnecessarily, and some will make you less capable of dealing with the setback successfully.

The main technique in *Antivirus For Your Mind* is to look at your explanation and see if you've made any thought-mistakes.

If you then find mistakes in your explanation, you will naturally form new explanations of the setback.

The question for today (What would be a more reasonable explanation?) goes straight to the task of creating a new explanation. You can use the question as a sort of shortcut to the antivirus technique once you've trained yourself to detect mistakes in your explanations. You can also use this question if you don't have time to look for mistakes and want a quick and dirty method. After a setback occurs, notice the explanation you automatically made for it, and then ask yourself what would be a more reasonable explanation.

For example, let's say you have a goal to make ten thousand dollars this month but by the end of the month, you didn't achieve your goal. This is a failure, and you will explain it automatically. Let's say you explain it like this: "The economy isn't doing very well right now."

But then you use today's question. You ask yourself, "Is there a more *reasonable* explanation?" Not that there is anything horribly wrong with your first explanation. It's that not bad. It takes the blame off yourself, so it'll keep you from feeling too bad about it. But on the other hand, the explanation leaves you somewhat powerless. It doesn't give you any avenue for finding a way to make ten thousand dollars when the economy is doing poorly, which leaves you somewhat helpless in the face of forces outside yourself.

So you try to think of another explanation (something *true*). "I didn't do all I planned on doing. Maybe that's why I didn't hit my target of ten thousand dollars." This explanation gives you an avenue to pursue that might actually lead to you achieving your goal next month regardless of what the economy is doing.

It's always good to come up with more than one alternative explanation. So you try again. "I wasted a lot of time on the least profitable part of my business. If I eliminated that part of my business, I would have more time for the more profitable things." Again, this could lead to actions that might make you more capable of hitting your goal next month.

Every failure is probably influenced by many different factors. Trying to come up with alternative explanations opens your mind to factors in your power to control, and that not only makes you feel better, it makes you more capable of changing things in the future.

If an event happens and you feel bad about it, your feelings derive largely from how you explained the event. And your ability to deal with the setback is influenced by the way you explained it to yourself. However reasonable your automatic explanation is, can you think of an even better explanation? If you can, it will change your feelings and your capabilities.

What Emotion Am I Aiming For?

One of the problems with the positive thinking literature is its obsession with cheerfulness and enthusiasm, which often translates into *acting* cheerful or enthusiastic, which often translates into being *phony*. And being phony doesn't feel good. That's one way "trying to be positive" short-circuits itself. But cheerfulness and enthusism are not the only two positive or worthwhile emotions. Many other emotions are superior, especially around other people. It can be annoying for other people when you are acting cheerful and enthusiastic when they don't feel that way at all. Especially if they suspect you're faking it.

But nobody would be annoyed if you were cultivating the feeling of *affection* or *kindness*. Those are also positive emotions. And they focus your attention outside yourself.

Another good emotion to aim for is *calmness*. Another is a feeling of *determination*.

Once you know what emotion you're trying to cultivate, it will influence what you do. When you're aiming for calmness, for example, you will probably change your posture a little, and maybe change the way you breathe. You might take deep breaths more often. You'll speak differently. Trying to cultivate calmness might change the way you're thinking and the way you treat people. You might try to stay relaxed and when you notice your neck muscles are tense, you might deliberately relax them. And the result of all these efforts will be: You'll feel more calm and relaxed.

Whatever emotion you cultivate influences you. Most of us want to be "a more positive person." And that's admirable. It would make the world a better place. It would make us personally happier. But let's do it in a way that *feels good* inside. And let's do it in a way that helps others feel good too. Think about the possible positive emotions, and choose to cultivate the ones you really like. W. Clement Stone liked enthusiasm and showed us how to cultivate it. Napoleon Hill liked cheerfulness and showed us how to cultivate it. What emotions do *you* like?

The Best Question to Ask

You've read the questions. That's the end of the list. But I'm not quite finished with this powerful topic. I have a little coaching for you on the way you use questions to direct your mind. The first piece of advice is to make sure your questions do not have the word "why" in them.

A woman named Vivian wrote to me and told me she had trouble sleeping. She had four kids and she was worried some day she would commit suicide. I was telling her about this principle of asking questions, and she tried it the very next night. But the question she pondered all night was, "Why do I think I'm destined for suicide?"

Vivian said, "I was up all night answering myself! I thought of answer after answer. The list went on and on, each answer breeding more questions of its own."

I told her that generally "how" questions work much better than "why" questions. She had been suffering from insomnia for a long time. But the very next night after she learned about the difference between "why" questions and "how" questions, she asked herself, "How can I prevent myself from ending up a suicide?" and she thought of so many good answers so quickly, she relaxed and fell asleep and slept longer than she had in a very long time.

The next day I told her about studies on suicide showing that people with suicidal thoughts who don't commit suicide had a reason to live. That sounds so obvious it seems almost ridiculous someone had to do an experiment to prove it. The reasons people had (reasons to live) varied quite a bit. Some people didn't kill themselves only because it would be too painful for their sister, or it was against their religion, or they had some purpose they wanted to fulfill. But the difference between those who stayed alive and those who killed themselves was simple: The people who had a reason to live did not kill themselves.

The next day, Vivian was thinking about that study and she realized she really wanted to see her boys grow up. She had four sons, the oldest was 13. She said, "I have thought before that I'm here because they need me, but it felt like an obligation. But I've realized I really *want* to see my sons grow up to be old men."

That is a potent realization. I'm sure you can easily grasp the tremendous difference in motivation, determination, and power between an obligation and a genuine, sincere, deeply-felt desire.

So now she had a goal, a reason to live, and the thought was on her mind for a few days, when she told me, "I like to watch them and think about them 'then' and 'now' and now I wonder what they'll be like when they're older. It's a surprise I don't want to miss. This very thought has been in my mind the past couple of days...it's a surprise I don't want to miss.' It's exciting and motivating."

Do you see what happened? She had a new question she was asking. "I wonder what my kids will be like when they're older?" Her question was purposeful (since she can influence the outcome) and forward-looking. And it directly counters the thought of suicide, doesn't it? She'll miss the surprise if she kills herself. It's a question that can't be answered now. She has to stay alive to see the answer. Brilliant, really.

She was already asking questions without realizing it. We all are. She started doing it deliberately and stopped asking herself "why" questions and it totally changed the direction and tone of her life.

It can work the same magic for you. Why not start today? Wait, change that to: "How can you start today?"

Coaching on Asking a Good Question

Y ou now know why you should use questions to direct your mind. But before I leave this important topic, I wanted to give you another good method for asking questions. It entails using another all-purpose tool: Making a list. A good way to use the power of asking a question is ask it on paper and make a list of answers. Ask the question and keep writing down answers. Set some kind of target — 100 answers, for example — and don't stop until you hit the target. I think you'll be surprised at some of the things you come up with, and maybe surprised at how creative you can be.

Or set a timer for a period of time, say an hour, and keep coming up with answers until the timer beeps. Pick one question, set your alarm, and jot down as many answers to the question as you can in that time. Don't monitor your answers or judge them (yet). Just try to answer the question as creatively as you can.

The first few answers will be normal, predictable answers. But then you'll run out of those, and your creativity will have to kick in.

When your time is up, go through and pick the best answers.

A freeform question-and-answer session can be productive too. By "freeform" I mean to ask whatever question comes up for you, and then answer it to the best of your ability. Then see what question comes up for you next, and then answer that one.

For example, this little freeform dialog happened when my first book was published and I was trying to get it for sale in bookstores. I hit several setbacks in a row and I was feeling disheartened. Yet the written dialog I had with myself lifted me out of my depressed state within minutes. I felt strong and determined after-wards. My fighting spirit returned.

Q: Why do I feel sad and defeated?

A: It seems like all I do is stick my neck out, then people are mean to me, and then I feel like a loser.

Q: Why do I want to promote this book?

A: I want Klassy proud of me. I want to make a difference with my life. I want to sell lots of books. I want to make money.

Q: Would I be willing to gain those things if I had to pay for it by sticking my neck out, having some people be mean to me, and occasionally feeling like a loser?

A: Yes. Absolutely.

In that short time, I suddenly felt determined. My motivation came back. I remembered that every person I admired had experienced similar trials and hardships, and my line of questioning cast my setbacks in a new, more inspiring context.

The primary way of asking questions is to create a good question and then have it on your mind for several days or weeks, pondering it in your spare time. It's a good way to direct your mind, motivate yourself, increase your determination, and make lasting changes.

But the two variations I mention in this chapter can work more *quickly*. Either ask a question and challenge yourself to make a list of answers, or use a free-form question-and-answer technique. Any questions?

The List Of Questions

1. What am I grateful for?
2. If I was happy about this, what would I be thinking about it?
3. What did I do right today?
4. What CAN I change?
5. Does this help my goal?
6. What does life expect from me?
7. How can I prevent this from ever happening again?
8. What is the best use of my time right now?
9. How can I use this to accomplish my goal?
10. What's good about this?
11. What is my goal here?

12. What is another way to look at this?

13. What else?

14. What memory makes me feel good?

15. Ask questions to find out more about the situation.

16. What if it really happened?

17. What am I good at?

18. What is one healthy thing I could do today to feel better?

19. What needs to be done next?

20. What good have I been ignoring?

21. How can I look at this as a good thing?

22. What could I do to make some progress on my goal?

23. Could I just do part of it for now?

24. What would be a more reasonable explanation?

25. What emotion am I aiming for?

About the Author

Adam Khan is the author of the books, *Cultivating Fire, Antivirus For Your Mind, Fill Your Tank With Freedom, Self-Reliance Translated, How to Change the Way You Look at Things (in Plain English), Slotralogy, Self-Help Stuff That Works, Principles For Personal Growth,* and *What Difference Does It Make?*

Adam blogs at adamlikhan.com and podcasts at The Adam Bomb.

Adam has been published in Prevention Magazine, Cosmopolitan, Body Bulletin, Wisdom, Your Personal Best Newsletter, Think and Grow Rich Newsletter, the Success Strategies newsletter, and he was a regular columnist for *At Your Best* (a Rodale Press publication) for seven years where his monthly column was voted the readers' favorite. Write to him at adamkhan@usa.com.

www.ingramcontent.com/pod-product-compliance
Lightning Source LLC
Chambersburg PA
CBHW021156020426
42331CB00003B/89